SUCCEEDING
WITH
CONSULTANTS

Self-Assessment for the
Changing Nonprofit

BARBARA KIBBE and FRED SETTERBERG
for The David and Lucile Packard Foundation

PUBLISHED BY THE FOUNDATION CENTER

To our courageous friends, colleagues,
and clients,
whose work is essential and invaluable

Library of Congress Cataloging-in-Publication Data

Kibbe, Barbara.
    Succeeding with consultants : self-assessment for the changing nonprofit/
Barbara Kibbe, Fred Setterberg for the David and Lucile Packard Foundation.
        p.   cm.
    ISBN 0-87954-450-3 : $14.95
        1. Corporations, Nonprofit–Management.   2. Consultants.
I. Setterberg, Fred.   II. David & Lucile Packard Foundation.   III. Title
HD62.6.K53   1992
    658.4′6–dc20   92-9330
                                                                                            CIP

TABLE OF CONTENTS

FOREWORD

The Board of Trustees and the program staff of The David and Lucile Packard Foundation view the Management Assistance Program as a service to our grantee organizations and the constituents they serve. It was in this spirit of service that this manual was conceived and created. We hope it will enable organizations to see problems and dilemmas as the challenges they present and to begin addressing those challenges positively and humanely. The tools in this manual represent practical ways for the board and staff of nonprofit organizations to assess management capacity and to begin a dialogue about what may be working and what may not be working. The consultant information represents guidelines for helping to make the consultant/client relationship work more effectively. Both the tools and the consultant components of the manual grew out of the foundation's work with organizations over the last decade, and the tools were further developed through a series of focus groups.

On behalf of the Packard Foundation trustees and staff, we thank all of those involved in the creation of this project, particularly the dedicated staff of the many agencies who gave their time and the outstanding consultants who designed, coordinated, wrote, and rewrote this manual.

Colburn S. Wilbur
Executive Director

Geri Rivard
Senior Program Officer

PREFACE

The nonprofit sector experienced rapid change during the last decade. More change will undoubtedly occur as demand for service escalates, support and subsidies dwindle, and the Internal Revenue Service looks more and more closely at nonprofits' income-generating strategies. The sector, quite simply, is caught in a squeeze brought about by larger economic pressures.

In our consulting and in preparing the tools and manuscript for *Succeeding with Consultants*, we work with the belief that individuals filling the roles of nonprofit executive or board member must balance flexibility with a clear sense of purpose.

Success in the context of constant change and challenge also depends on these individuals possessing a broad array of technical information and skills. Yet no one is born knowing what will be required of them in these roles. In fact, on-the-job training is the norm rather than the exception.

With all that in mind, we have designed what we hope is a package of practical educational tools for the nonprofit sector and its devoted servants and advocates.

Our first and most heartfelt thanks go to the champion of this project, Geri Rivard. As this book goes to press, she is entering her ninth year at the David and Lucile Packard Foundation, first as a consultant and since 1985 as a program officer. Her belief in the sector and its power to change the world for the better led her to develop the foundation's Management Assistance Program in conjunction with the foundation's executive director and board of trustees.

In addition, literally hundreds of individuals and organizations helped and supported this enterprise. Their commitment and continuing encouragement were felt at every phase of the lengthy process of developing *Succeeding with Consultants* and from the entire foundation—from its founder, David Packard, and its capable executive director, Colburn Wilbur, to other program and support staff.

Numerous focus groups drew on the energy, expertise, and generosity of board and staff members from a diverse array of nonprofit organizations. Some of these devoted professionals participated in groups facilitated by the authors prior to developing each diagnostic tool. Others spent some of their all too scarce time testing the tools and making suggestions for improvements.

We also wish to thank our colleagues in the field of nonprofit consulting whose expert review and comments (and sometimes cajoling) helped us to finish what we sincerely hope will prove to be an asset for the sector. First is Paul Harder—colleague, partner, friend, and quality assurance maven who, six years ago, conducted the foundation's Management Assistance Program evaluation and uncovered the growing need for guidance in using consultants.

Alice Ito supported both Paul and Geri in the program evaluation, ultimately drafting materials about nonprofit consultants that became the inspiration for our "consumer's guide." Susan Colson's contribution as tireless reviewer of a mountain of existing diagnostic materials was invaluable as was her careful assistance in field-testing the first tools produced. Renee Lagloire's contribution as focus group transcriber, and additional analytical mind is felt on every page of *Succeeding with Consultants*. Thanks also go to Joycelyn Moulton for her help with logistics, and to Jan Masaoka for her thoughtful and frank discussion about the consulting business.

Our expert reviewers included a distinguished list of accomplished trainers, authors, foundation executives, and consultants. Their perspectives often broadened our own view and understanding of the sector. And finally, the authors want to pay special tribute to a few unique contributors to the project: Eden Tanovitz, Susan Avila, Victoria Kirby, and Mark Jansen.

Thank you all.

Barbara Kibbe

Fred Setterberg

PART I
. . . .

Preparing For Change

YOU'VE GOT A PROBLEM. BUT–WHAT IS IT?
Confronting the daily dynamics of nonprofit life

"Confusion now hath made his masterpiece!"
– Shakespeare, *Macbeth*

In the complicated world of nonprofit organizations, it can seem like everything goes wrong at once.

Good staff people quit. Funding withers away. Volunteers place their energy elsewhere – and your best programs may refuse to grow. Over the past decade, as harsh political and economic realities have put more and more pressure on nonprofits, we've also adjusted for increased consumer demand, uncertain spending priorities, and complicated and dispiriting new social problems.

These changes have placed great stress upon our organizations, often undermining efforts to solve our own internal problems.

Today many nonprofit managers and board members find themselves facing an extraordinary number of fundamental management questions. As a result, they may end up making a very understandable, but deadly mistake: They confuse symptoms with root causes.

They'll mix up their immediate problem – for example, nobody shows up for a board meeting – with the organizational issues that lie behind it.

In the case of phantom board members, the root cause *might* be:

- poor communication about the time, date, or place of the meeting.

- hopeless directions to the meeting site.

- too many other responsibilities stacked upon the board members' weary (and resentful) shoulders.

- lack of clarity about the reasons for holding board meetings in the first place.

- rapid turnover in membership, eroding the board's reliable core.

- confusion regarding board responsibilities.

- fundamental disagreement over the organization's main goal and, thus, the board's role in achieving it.

- covert actions on the part of a board faction ready to mount an insurrection.

- highly charged personal feelings about the board president or executive director – almost certainly masking other substantive and suppressed organizational issues.

In short, the problem of poor attendance at board meetings could be the reflection of any one of several organizational maladies – or a dizzying mixture of many. By itself, poor attendance tells us little more than that there is, in fact, a problem.

Of course, most nonprofit executives, staff, board members, and volunteers want nothing more than to end the management troubles that undermine their patience, commitment, and sanity. But organizations are more complicated than that.

In fact, most nonprofit groups revel in complexity. They're a lot like living organisms – they breathe, they contain mystery. When something goes wrong, the reasons are often obscure, even in healthy, established groups. Factors such as individual personalities, timing, organizational history, and outside economic and political forces (that you probably can't control) make off-the-cuff diagnoses of management problems extremely difficult – and potentially dangerous.

Careful, deliberate assessments carried out internally or assisted by the outside perspective of a consultant can often transform conflicts or perplexing problems into a concrete plan to enhance the health and effectiveness of your organization.

YOUR NONPROFIT GROWS UP

Not all problems portend organizational disaster – or even ill health. Organizational life is a constant process of evolution and revolution. The movement from stage to stage – like our own personal journeys from childhood to adolescence, from adolescence to adulthood – seldom proves carefree and easy.

Organizational Development (OD) is the name given to a field of study (and also a discipline of consulting) that analyzes the interplay of many forces and factors affecting organizational change and growth.

OD specialists can identify a multiplicity of stages of organizational growth that reflect healthy change. At every stage, you will almost certainly find special developmental challenges that must be met – or else the evolutionary process will be stalled.

We've simplified the shifts for purposes of discussion, looking at only four of the possible (and very different) stages in the lives of nonprofits.

- *Infancy.* In the life of a nonprofit, this "start-up" phase is a time of immediate response to stimuli. This period, which can last months or years, may seem like a time of constant crisis as policies and practices are created to meet each new challenge. The founders' vision is usually clear at this stage, although the route to attaining it may remain mysterious. Seen in its most positive light, organizational infancy is a time of building precedent. It is also a time of enormous enthusiasm where even small successes are noticed, appreciated, and hailed.

- *Youth.* The shift from infancy to youth might occur when a group's founder or first charismatic leader departs. When organizations of any age lose their charismatic leader, they typically face a wide range of management issues. This is only logical, because the leader who provides the initial burst of energy and direction is often a visionary – but rarely an efficient manager who wants to establish operational systems for the long haul. In an organization's youth, you can expect an increasing emphasis on accountability as the new emerging leadership attempts to inject stability and durability into their organization. Some groups falter here, unable to sustain energy or to develop needed resources in the face of their departing founder or depleting seed money.

- *Early adulthood.* Stability characterizes this stage in a nonprofit's life. Unfortunately, boredom may come along with it. The nonprofit in its early adulthood needs to feel young again. Once efficient management systems have been set in place are functioning, organizations must contend with an almost inevitable deflation and loss of energy. The challenge here is to regain some of the original spirit that gave birth to the organization – and integrate this spirit into daily operations.

- *Maturity.* It's no accident that this phase is often called *institutionalization.* A crisis can occur in the life of a mature organization when the well-structured and vital organization rouses up its courage to reevaluate its fundamental mission. After years of operation, and even success, the institutional nonprofit needs to determine whether it's truly making progress toward achieving its long-term goals or just coasting on past achievements.

All of these phases and their attendant crises occur naturally with the passage of time. Other life-threatening crises can and often do disrupt the natural evolution of organizational life. Whether you are dealing with the challenges of guiding a nonprofit from one developmental state to another or facing a challenge to the very existence of your organization, its health can be enhanced by organizational self-scrutiny.

LEARNING TO LIVE WITH CHANGE
Anticipating resistance from within

"All things change; nothing perishes."

– Ovid

"Keep what you have; the known evil is best," advised Plautus, the comic playwright of classical Rome.

Better the devil you know than the devil you don't know, we say in the United States.

It all adds up to the same thing: We hate change.

Revolutionary zeal in planning for the future – an absolute necessity for nonprofits – will stir up the full range of highly emotional and personal, as well as logical, reasons why human beings battle change:

- added job responsibilities – probably without increased pay.

- higher stress.

- disruption of comfortable routines.

- dread of uncertain outcomes.

- the burden of acquiring new skills and knowledge.

- personality conflicts with new supervisors, co-workers, or board members.

- fears about inadequacy, making mistakes, or being "found out" in an altered work environment.

Of course, all of these disasters won't befall most organizations. But fear is not entirely bounded by rational thought. Fear is a survival mechanism. If your staff has experienced unwieldy change in the past, you can bet that they'll either gallop straight away from the process you want to initiate, or they'll stand and fight. But needs and insecurities of individuals inside your organization will not constitute the only point of resistance.

Once you begin to broadcast your intentions for change, you'll soon find that the organization has a stubborn life of its own. In its own eccentric way, *it* will exert subtle, powerful influences to resist your tinkering with its momentum and equilibrium.

When your ambitious plan for improvement intrudes upon the organizational status quo, you can bet that life is going to get even more complicated.

By raising the possibility of change, you'll almost certainly dredge up a great number of complex, related issues. Staff needs, personal agendas, and organizational inertia will all rise to a head. And they'll combine with the everyday difficulties of maturing, both individually and organizationally, to present even greater challenges to the resiliency and determination of your group.

These challenges are normal and inevitable.

But most nonprofit professionals find great difficulty in juggling the realistic, exaggerated, and sometimes even imaginary concerns of their board and staff during a time of change.

MAKING CHANGE

As the person advocating change, you'll sometimes be facing a lonely task. But that doesn't mean you should work alone.

Successful organizational change always occurs through intense collaboration. To create a collaborative environment, relying on the strength of varied opinions and perspectives, you'll need:

- a process for unearthing information – much of it gleaned from your colleagues and board members.

- a blame-free, open attitude that encourages people to speak their minds without fear of future penalty.

- a willingness to benefit from the wisdom of the group.

The help of an outside consultant can prove invaluable in orchestrating positive change.

READ BEFORE USING

Part II offers a thorough, step-by-step method for working with a consultant to identify and solve your problems. The idea of working with a consultant may be greeted with a combination of suspicion and skepticism within your organization.

Pay attention to these concerns. Beneath them lie genuine issues. In any case, the predictable anxieties of your staff and board should once again raise this key question: Why do you want to hire a consultant, and what do you expect the consultant to accomplish?

It will also be useful for the consultant, presuming he or she is finally hired, to hear about the organization's misgivings. Skepticism is healthy and inevitable. A responsible organization won't enter lightly into a consulting agreement.

Of course, it would allay everybody's fears if you could precisely enumerate the accomplishments that the consultant will achieve and the benefits to be gained *before* you begin. But that's not always possible unless the task is a limited project, like designing a brochure, and maybe not even then. A successful consulting relationship often resembles a detective's investigation.

Perhaps your most strategic option is to nudge your board and staff toward a more general admission of the obvious: You've got a problem, and you need outside assistance to solve it. If you're advocating a consultant to intervene, make it clear that you're not trying to undermine the authority of the board or staff, you don't secretly want to fire somebody, and you don't think it's

time to lock up the office and call it quits. You just need help.

Try to employ a generous language of collective responsibility: Remind everybody that it's still *"our* organization." *We've* got the power, and together *we'll* determine how best to work with this mysterious outsider, the consultant.

The point here is to make certain that your board and staff feel, and indeed *are,* involved in the consulting process from the very beginning. Otherwise, you'll eventually find yourself trying to bully key people into cooperation, which will prove disastrous. Keep in mind the character in George Bernard Shaw's play *Man and Superman,* whose friends worry that she'll do "just exactly as she likes. And what's more, she'll force us to advise her to do it; and she'll put the blame on us if it turns out badly." In their worst nightmares, your board and staff share this fear when the "wily" consultant steps through the door.

In the pages following, we'll examine the best strategies for insuring your organization's success in the consulting process.

Part III of *Succeeding with Consultants* consists of an extensive set of diagnostic tools that can assist you (and/or your consultant) in diagnosing and addressing organizational problems. The tools can be adopted by your consultant—or you can use them on your own.

Remember that self-assessment is not a textbook exercise; it takes place in the real world. Some organizations will find it extremely difficult to grapple with their own organizational history in order to pick up the information and analysis required for a clear self-assessment. And they'll find it harder yet to transform their point of view into consensus—and consensus into collective action. But, year after year, in organization after organization, *it is done!*

You may want to begin the repairs today by picking up these tools.

Or if you believe that such a task would prove absolutely impossible for your organization as it stands today, then you should seriously think seriously about working with a consultant to help you over barriers.

PART II

Working With A Consultant

REACHING OUT

Do you really need a consultant – and what is one, anyway?

"If there are obstacles, the shortest line between two points may be the crooked one."
— Bertolt Brecht

Skeptical managers in the business world and in the nonprofit sector enjoy telling each other that the frank, clear-eyed definition of a consultant is:

1. somebody who borrows your watch to tell you the time (and then walks off with the watch).

2. somebody who knows a thousand ways to make love, but never has any dates.

3. somebody who's chronically unemployed, but wants to be paid an extravagant fee while sizing up your organization for the job that he or she should never be offered.

These are harsh words for consulting and consultants, but ones worth keeping in mind when you're thinking about hiring a consultant. A little healthy skepticism can banish the aura of invulnerability in which many consultants have cloaked themselves.

It can also focus your sights upon that essential question: What is a consultant—and can one help *me*?

In the nonprofit sector, a good consultant usually turns out to be a teacher—and a student. Also a problem-solver and a fountain of good advice... not to mention a walking library of nuts-and-bolts information. Sometimes the consultant must assume the alternating role of diplomat and tough guy. Then again, it may be important for the consultant to play conscience and cheerleader... as well as therapist, surgeon, private investigator, and advocate.

The nonprofit consultant's role is complex. Consultants may be called upon to train board and staff or conduct independent research and analysis. They may spearhead an executive search, diagnose management problems, mediate conflicts between organizational factions, or facilitate meetings to start planning for the future. Consultants help develop new systems for computers, marketing, fiscal oversight, fund development, and every other task facing the average nonprofit. It's because of this complexity and variety that the consultant's role is often misunderstood.

In a phrase, a consultant offers you advice, perspective, tools, inspiration, skills, and time you don't have to help you solve your own problems.

WHY HIRE A CONSULTANT?

In addition to an abundance of bad reasons (which we'll get to shortly), there are typically three good reasons to hire a consultant:

- *You have a specific task that must be accomplished.* You and your staff have neither the time nor skill to tackle the job alone. Perhaps you need a new computer system selected, installed, and the proper people trained to use it. Or you finally resolve to implement the accounting procedures that you've painfully lacked over the past ten years, or any number of other specific tasks requiring expertise that once completed, produce a calculable benefit.

- *You've got a problem.* Perhaps you can identify it. ("Our board doesn't know how to fundraise.") Maybe you can't. ("As executive director, I never seem to have time to complete the important jobs. How come?") A consultant can help you unravel the question and develop an approach or an answer to it.

- *You've got a problem and you know how to solve it—but you can't motivate your board or staff to take action.* In this case the skilled consultant serves as a catalyst for group commitment, rousing up enthusiasm and conviction where the all too familiar executive director may simply invite skepticism and indifference.

Unraveling Consulting

Every field has its own jargon. Consulting, perhaps because of the intangible nature of many of its features and goals, seems to have more than its fair share.

If you at first have difficulty understanding exactly what your consultant is proposing to do for you, then simply ask for a plain English translation. If you still don't understand, consider looking for a new consultant. If your "professional" can't describe his or her profession from the outset—or if you can't grasp it—then further collaboration may be hopeless.

Of course it won't hurt for you to become familiar with the common professional terms.

Here then, in the original "consultese" and followed by an English translation, are the most common tasks that consultants undertake in the nonprofit world:

1. *Diagnosis and assessment:* They'll identify your problems with you and state them.

2. *Problem solving:* They'll suggest ways of solving your problems.

3. *Research and analysis:* They'll investigate the trends, events, obstacles, and opportunities affecting your organization's goals.

4. *Training:* They'll teach your board and staff essential skills, such as volunteer supervision or fundraising.

5. *Mediation:* They'll help resolve disputes with or within your organization.

6. *Facilitation:* They'll help set goals for an important meeting, such as an annual retreat or membership meeting, and lead group members through a series of structured steps to meet the goals.

7. *Contract services:* They'll hire out to plan and execute high-skill tasks of limited duration, such as conducting a marketing survey or publicity campaign.

8. *Systems development:* They'll devise reliable methods for conducting daily business, such as financial accounting systems, or they may concentrate on providing the best available equipment—including computers and software—to accomplish important tasks.

9. *Executive search:* They'll locate candidates to fill your executive director position, or other key staff slots.

10. *Organizational process:* They'll help identify and resolve problems in communication, personnel conflict, and collaboration that hinder you from attaining your organizational goals.

11. *Planning:* They'll work with the board to devise and complete a strategy for the organization's future.

12. *Fund development:* They'll assist board and staff in developing strategies for fundraising or in carrying out fundraising plans.

13. *Board development:* They'll help you identify goals for your board, help you plan to recruit new members, and train the board to meet their goals.

In practice consultants rarely take on just one of the tasks outlined here. A good consultant can and often will work on several fronts simultaneously and comfortably.

Traits of a Good Consultant

Because of the immense variation found in the consulting role and lack of licensing or other widely accepted standards of qualification, it's difficult to talk about precise and objective standards of competence. Yet while no two consultants work in exactly the same way, all capable professionals will demonstrate three essential qualities.

Skill. Most consultants develop specialties: clusters of related skills, like fundraising and planning or board development and staff training. They keep up with developments in the field by studying the new literature, staying in touch with colleagues, and consistently re-examining their own theories, biases, and experience. Their professional credibility is based upon their consistent ability to perform at an exceptionally high level in the areas that they have embraced as their own.

Sensitivity. Consulting is very often group work. Good consultants relish the complexity of group behavior. They anticipate the problems that inevitably crop up during any kind of collective endeavor. And they know how to harness the energy of the group, without turning the process into a therapy session or allowing it to disintegrate.

Experience. Good consultants have track records. They won't be using your organization as though it were a highly paid internship to learn the fundamentals of nonprofit management. Your organization's problems will neither shock nor frighten the seasoned consultant. They've seen and done it all before.

FOUR TERRIBLE WAYS TO USE A CONSULTANT

Part of the reason for the consultant's recent popularity in the nonprofit world is economic. New funding sources have not sprung up to offset the cost of rising wages. In fact competition for funding has become even more fierce. And because nonprofits are no longer exempt from participation in the Social Security system (FICA taxes), there's an added incentive to reduce payroll expenses by hiring part-time, contract-based labor. The high turnover rate in the nonprofit sector has also forced more nonprofits to rely on expert outsiders who need not be trained at the expense of the organization. Finally, the difficulty in firing staff, fueled by the fear of retaliatory lawsuits, has given consultants an extra edge.

But as consultants gain popularity in the nonprofit sector, there's also been an attendant rise in confusion over their proper role. Following are the four most common ways that consultants are now misused.

Consultant as Fall Guy

If you're going to benefit from the consultant process, then you must be prepared to understand and act upon advice that may strike a sensitive nerve. Consultants sometimes get blamed for the problems they've merely identified. And when a consultant departs under a cloud, he or she can carry with her all hope for mobilizing forces for change within the organization.

Consultant as Hit Man

Sometimes the only viable solution to an organizational ill is to fire somebody. While consultants may raise the question about staff performance, they should *never* be given – or accept – the task of actually firing someone. That's your responsibility.

Consultant as Messiah

The best consultants exude confidence, wisdom, and understanding – qualities that we'd all like to display in abundance. But keep in mind that the consultant wants to *inspire* as well as advise you. Capitalize on whatever charismatic power your consultant may possess to motivate you and your colleagues, but don't confuse his or her flair with infallibility. Nobody benefits if the consultant is deemed all-powerful and all-knowing.

Consultant as Burden

Bringing in a consultant may be *one* person's "bright idea." It may even be suggested by a funder as part of (or preliminary to) an approved grant to aid some new endeavor. The consultant's presence, under these circumstances, can feel like a gift, or it can feel coerced. If working with the consultant is half-hearted, the consulting process is unlikely to yield good results.

HOW TO WORK WITH CONSULTANTS

Many nonprofit executives feel overburdened by the enormous variety of tasks that they're expected to perform. And the same can be said of nonprofit boards. Why should we presume that a volunteer board of parents, shopkeepers, lawyers, and mechanics should know the first thing about the intricacies of needs assessment, direct-mail fundraising, or program evaluation?

No matter how predictable, these gaps in knowledge mean that the board and staff in most organizations waste a tremendous amount of time trying to address their problems with solutions that were already refined by others. The good consultant can stop you from re-inventing the wheel.

But the consultant is only half of the equation. The attitudes and behavior of key people in your organization will also shape consultant experience. Before your board and staff even meet the consultant, you can take steps to promote the best possible working relationship by exploding the three following common myths:

Myth #1: A Consultant Will Do the Work for You

No myth is more pervasive. And so this warning bears repetition: A good consultant doesn't take over essential staff and board responsibilities; rather, he or she guides *you* in diagnosing, evaluating, and solving your own problems. At the end of the relationship, you're not merely left with the memory of a job well done. You'll also possess the skill and experience to tackle similar problems when they turn up in the future—which they will.

Of course some consultants are specifically contracted to handle a single or ongoing task necessary for your group's continued health. But generally this task will be unrelated to deeper issues of governance, management, purpose, and strategy. Some consultants grapple with the tasks that your board and staff *shouldn't* have to worry about. (You may need that new computer system, but nobody in the organization really has to submerge him or herself in the deep-sea world of hardware and software. That's why you hire the consultant. . . .)

Myth #2: The Consultant Can Do It Alone

The best consultants affect organizations at their core. They introduce new systems. They impart information that improves job performance. When they have something important to say, there's somebody on the other side of the table who's listening. They engage board and staff in an ongoing conversation about goals that leads to action *and* change. A group of people cannot be tricked, bullied, or forced into organizational transformation. But they can be encouraged, and *that's* a good reason to hire a consultant.

Myth #3: Change Will Come Quickly

There probably will be some quick changes. (Along the lines of the consultant's advice, you could set up a new bookkeeping system almost immediately.) But the real strength in the consulting process involves deeper, more fundamental changes that will become apparent only over a period of months. (With time, your new bookkeeping system should reflect a more prudent overall approach to financial management that's also characterized by improved board fundraising and planning for long-range fund development.)

Keep in mind that the best consultant will not be able to change your organization's basic values. And the most dynamic consulting process won't alter the personalities or worldview of the board and staff. But with new tools and perspective at their disposal, board and staff should find themselves tempted to think and act in new ways.

IMPOSTORS AND EXPERTS
How to find, select, and hire the right consultant

"Your doubt may be a good quality if you train it."
— Rainer Maria Rilke

Once you've clarified your purpose in searching for outside help, it's time to get started. But where do you find a consultant?

Today they seem to be everywhere. In the United States, more than 3,500 consulting firms now operate, with many times that number of individual consultants lurking throughout the major metropolitan areas. The Association of Consulting Management Firms estimates that fees paid to management consultants have hit the $6 billion range—with $2.5 billion spent by public-sector clients.

Small and midsized nonprofits are best advised to begin the search for skilled and experienced consultants close to home.

- You'll find them in the classified pages of non-profit management assistance magazines such as *Fund Raising Management* or *Foundation News*. You might even comb the pages of your local telephone directory.

- You can contact local chapters of professional consultant organizations specializing in nonprofit concerns, such as the National Society of Fund Raising Executives (NSFRE).

- Or you might turn to your local United Way office or staffed foundations for referrals to consultants with whom they've worked in the past.

You should also talk with other nonprofit groups in your community that have recently hired and worked with a consultant. In fact, this contact should mark the beginning of an extended conversation that will continue throughout the course of the consulting process.

Your aim is to become an expert consumer. And your best resource will be your more experienced peers.

In short, getting names is easy. Making choices is hard.

Once you've uncovered a number of prospective consultants, the real work begins. Now you must separate the genuine from the phony, the expert from the unemployed.

Of course this isn't a new problem. Whenever you hire a staff person, the same kind of judgments come into play. Selecting a consultant is no more difficult—although it's no easier, either. You're searching for an expert in the field who can demonstrate excellence.

Unfortunately some organizations become intimidated by the prospect of interviewing the "expert." And in the process, they surrender their power, lose track of their goals, and hire the wrong people.

These are the five most common mistakes nonprofit groups make in selecting a consultant:

1. *Purchasing a parrot.* Some consultants are very skilled at deducing what nonprofit boards and executives want to hear from them. And they parrot back their client's worries, doubts, aspirations, and delusions, exhibiting great intuition and empathy. This situation requires careful discernment. One of the main reasons you're hiring a consultant is for the outsider's perspective, the neutrality of a disengaged expert who has nothing invested in maintaining the status quo. You already know what *you* think; why pay to hear it squawked back at you?

2. *Buying the whole pie.* No matter how devastating your organizational woes may be, you can take comfort in the fact that your needs aren't limitless; they're localized, finite. You don't need to know everything about the latest trends in artificial intelligence in order to install your new computer system. You just need to know what's going to work for you. Unfortunately, some consultants will be willing to provide you with far more than you need. And if you're willing to purchase the whole pie of their expertise when all you really need is a slice, then who can blame them for obliging?

3. *Solving the wrong problem.* Keep in mind that every consultant has something to sell—although it's not necessarily what you need to buy. "Redefining the problem is a consulting tactic of almost canonical stature," writes David Owen, "for the simple reason that it enables the consultant to set his own criteria for success or failure." In fact, the less experienced consultant may only have one skill that he or she has developed. In order to compensate for a lack of comprehensiveness, the consultant will learn to package that skill under a variety of names and guises. Or *you* may misunderstand the nature of your organization's problem and seek advice from the wrong person. For example, many organizations immediately consult fundraisers when they're having financial problems. In truth, the roots of their problem may require better financial reporting systems, clarified fiscal goals, a more vigorous board—and almost inevitably, a commitment to an extended planning process. Unfortunately the wrong or inexperienced consultant won't be able to lead a new client to this conclusion.

4. *Accepting the medical model.* Many consultants and clients like to use the language of medicine to describe their services and your problems. "When you bring the consultant in," wrote a respected practitioner from a major business consulting firm, "you will be more or less in the position of a doctor administering a promising new drug to a favorite patient."

But let's take a closer look at what can be a useful metaphor. The medical model of organizational consulting can imply an imbalance of power, particularly if the consultant's concept of a doctor is someone who does something *to* you rather than *with* you. Although radical surgery may be necessary at some point, the consultant's real gift to you will be more along the lines of preventive medicine—teaching you how to best care for yourself—so that you'll be able to ensure the vigorous longevity of your organization.

5. *False economies.* It's smart to save money. It's dumb to hire the wrong person in order to do it. Naturally you will want to secure bids from several consultants. But cheapest is not necessarily best. Nor are high fees a guarantee of good work. Because consultants deal in services—not products that have component parts that you can easily cost out and compare—it's possible to find price differences between firms running as high as 2,000 percent. Keep your eye on matching your needs with the best services available at a price you can truly afford.

LOOKING FOR MS. (OR MR.) RIGHT

It is imperative to interview more than one consultant. By doing so, you will quickly become acquainted with the range and variety of expertise available in your community. You'll begin to form opinions about what you value and what appears to be superfluous to your group's immediate and long-term needs.

The interview process isn't mysterious. You'll probably conduct it as you would for any other position that needs to be filled, involving a number of people from your organization to ensure perspective as well as support in making the choice.

Some useful questions to ask the candidates might include:

- Who have you worked for in the past, and what did you accomplish with them?

- Have you ever consulted on the same problem that our group now faces?

- What led you to consulting as a career?

- What is your work process? How would you collaborate with (or distance yourself from) the board, staff, and executive?

And finally, "You're the expert," you should inform the prospective consultant. "You tell me: what should I ask you about? How can I learn the most about how a consultant can help solve my problems?"

If the consultant seems promising after the personal interview, you should follow up by checking references. Ask for a client list, not the consultant's hand-picked batch of satisfied customers.

One of the great, unsolvable problems with reference checking is that fact that you'll be tracking client satisfaction—not the consultant's ultimate effectiveness in solving the organization's problems. Progress is far more difficult to measure than personal reactions to the consultant. A client may *feel* wonderful about the consulting experience, yet remain utterly unprepared to cope with the problems that first prompted him or her to seek outside help. Don't be satisfied with a vague, generalized review of the consultant's performance. Instead, you might ask the former clients you contact:

- Did the consultant quickly grasp the needs of your organization and its underlying problems?

- Was work completed on time and on schedule?

- Were changes in the workplan properly negotiated?

- Did the consultant work at an appropriate pace?

- How did the consultant's actions affect the board and staff?

- How did the consultant treat your staff? Did people like and respect the consultant?

- Would you hire the consultant again?

Finally, take a minute to describe why you're looking for a consultant and ask, "Do you think the consultant you used could help our organization with this problem?"

Keep in mind the three main qualities you're searching for: *skill, sensitivity,* and *experience,* and direct your inquiry to determining whether your candidates possess them.

If handled correctly, your choice of consultant will have a very positive effect on your organization. Because you plan to take action on the consultant's advice, you should be certain that you're hiring the right person.

Now is the time to review the reasons why you're seeking outside help. What changes do you want in your organization? How do you imagine that these changes might be fostered? What kind of consultant are you looking for—an organizational development specialist, fundraiser, technical expert? Good choices are usually the result of clarity about the aims and limitations of the consulting process combined with agreeable personal chemistry between the consultant and client. So, give equal time to gut feelings and to matching the skills of the consultant with the precise needs of the organization.

In the end you'll probably opt to hire a busy, but not overcommitted, professional. That person may work for a consulting firm or maintain an independent private practice. If you decide to engage a consulting firm, you'll benefit from the firm's support staff, reputation, and easily trackable performance record (all of which may convince reluctant board and staff that the changes you've been advocating make "good business sense"). On the other hand, you'll have to make certain that you get to work with the person you originally interviewed, aren't shunted from one staff consultant to another, and don't get lost among the firm's other (and perhaps higher-paying) clients. Also, independent consultants offer personal service and low overhead—although you may find that they have difficulty in maintaining adequate contact without a secretary and office. In the end, neither one nor the other can be considered innately superior. It's a matter of personal fit.

After an initial interview, the consultant should be asked to devise a proposal and workplan. This document will serve as a blueprint for the rest of the consulting process. It should spell out the problems and the goals of your collaboration, roundly sketching the activities to be pursued over a designated period of time.

You should provide the consultant with basic information about your organization prior to the consultant completing a workplan. Reading through a selection of reports, grants, budgets, minutes, and/or promotional materials can help your prospective helper to understand your needs better and will inevitably result in a more appropriate, thoughtful workplan.

In fact, some organizations disseminate a request for proposal (RFP) as a way to solicit consultants' interest in their project or problem. Such an RFP will offer information about the organization and the background of the project or problem its members would like the consultant to address. It also can be quite specific about the kind of written response you are looking for (e.g., qualifications, experience with similar projects and organizations, proposed workplan, timeline, and budget.) Whether you choose to issue an RFP or simply call in a number of consultants for interviews, a detailed workplan should be prepared by your consultant before beginning work—and it should be done free of charge.

The proposal and workplan should include:

- *background summary and goals* stating the problem to be solved or the objectives to be achieved.

- *approach and methods* to be used in reaching the goal.

- *tasks* to be undertaken, including details of each step.

- *personnel* responsible for accomplishing the tasks.

- *costs* for the entire project, broken down into logical categories.

- *a timeline* showing when the project will begin and end, as well as when major tasks will be undertaken along the way.

The proposal and workplan will enable you to grasp the consultant's approach quickly, evaluate his or her judgment, and introduce your own suggestions for work. It should serve as the primary tool for negotiating the details of the project, while further clarifying your own organizational goals. With time, you may have occasion to revise the workplan. And that's fine—as long as your revisions primarily focus upon methods, not objectives. Your objectives need to be agreed upon early in the process. The workplan is something like a map: Random, frequent goal shifting will quickly get you lost.

Following are two examples of a sample proposal, workplan, and timeline.

PROPOSAL TO ABC UNIVERSITY FOR MARKET RESEARCH, ANALYSIS, AND PLANNING

Introduction and Objectives

ABC University is experiencing a high rate of attrition among students. Because the university is almost completely tuition-based, questions about marketing and recruitment as well as student satisfaction are paramount in the minds of the university's Marketing and Communications departments.

Smith and Jones Research and Consulting has been asked to prepare a proposal that would address the information needs of ABC regarding current and potential future markets for their unique type of adult higher education.

We are here proposing a three-tiered effort aimed at assisting university planners and marketers in improving student retention, developing new enrollees and exploring new markets.

Preliminary objectives for the consultancy are:

1. to develop a more complete understanding of the characteristics/profile of current ABC students (i.e., the university's current market).

2. to discover the causes of the high rate of attrition among students.

3. to design measurable objectives for the university's future marketing and recruitment efforts.

4. to assist in developing/refining recruitment strategies.

5. to identify potential areas for successful program expansion (new markets).

6. to offer insights into cultivation of alumni involvement/support.

7. to support overall university planning.

Approach and Methods

The Smith and Jones approach to this project will involve a combination of data collection and analysis, focus groups, and facilitated meetings. We will place a high value on involving representatives from the university administration as well as faculty, students, alumni, and community leaders in both the research and the analysis/planning stages.

Workplan

What follows is a brief description of tasks to be undertaken by Smith and Jones. It should be noted, however, that this workplan was designed as a proposal only. It is possible that the emphasis will change based on a detailed discussion with the client prior to beginning work.

1. Student Survey

Our first task will be to design and administer a comprehensive survey of ABC students to create a picture of the university's current market. We will also test for the overall effectiveness of ABC's marketing messages, the degree to which students' expectations of the program are fulfilled once they are enrolled and their overall satisfaction with the university.

Data collected will be input into a database allowing for detailed analysis and cross-tabulations via personal computer within and among ABC's various schools and programs.

In drafting the survey analysis, we will take existing data – including the university's recently completed accreditation survey results – into account.

2. Focus Groups

Successful marketing strategies are often based on qualitative as well as quantitative research. In fact, some of the most creative ideas in marketing are the result of intuition.

Focus groups will provide a perspective unavailable from other data sources. Widely used in contemporary market research, the groups will allow deep insight into opinions and beliefs of selected participants while they also offer an opportunity for direct input into the research and planning process.

It is proposed that six focus groups be convened regarding each school. Participants will be chosen from among populations that represent current and potential markets for new students, potential employers of ABC graduates, alumni, and community leaders in areas where the university wants to encourage geographic expansion and possibly even experts in fields where the university is now actively engaged in training.

A transcript of each group session will be made available to the client along with summaries and analyses.

3. Develop Marketing Objectives and Strategies

With early involvement of key policymakers and implementers, setting objectives and developing strategies for the coming months and years should be fairly straightforward. We will plan a series of presentations and facilitated planning meetings with the following purposes: (1) to ensure that all persons intimately involved in the planning process are well informed about the results of the market research, and (2) to develop consensus on marketing objectives and strategies.

Our final report will include a summary of these meetings to serve as the basis for detailed action plans for each school.

Staffing and Project Management

Brenda Smith, principal of Smith and Jones Consulting, will direct this project. She will be responsible for designing the research process, conducting the analysis, leading focus groups and facilitating meetings. Ms. Smith's experience in nonprofit management consulting spans more than a decade and includes planning, meeting and focus group facilitation, feasibility studies, board and staff training, and public presentations. A complete resume and selected client list are enclosed.

Ms. Smith will be assisted by Ken Brown, research assistant with Smith and Jones. Mr. Brown will participate in survey administration, data entry, and focus group logistics.

Work Products

- Student survey instruments
- Transcripts of focus group sessions
- Summaries of facilitated meetings
- Final report including analysis of market research with recommendations

Budget

The time of the principal consultant will be charged at $75 per hour, the research assistant at $25 per hour. The tasks, time, and charges are estimated below.

Task	Hours	Charge
STUDENT SURVEY:		
Design and Implementation		
Principal	40	$ 3,000
Research Assistant	60	1,500
Data Entry and Analysis		
Principal	60	4,500
Research Assistant	120	3,000
Report and Presentation		
Principal	48	3,600
Expenses		
(postage, copying, phone, fax, local travel)		5,250
TOTAL SURVEY		$20,850

Task	Hours	Charge
FOCUS GROUPS:		
Design and Logistics		
Principal	32	$ 2,400
Research Assistant	80	2,000
Facilitation and Analysis		
Principal	120	9,000
Report and Presentation		
Principal	40	3,000
Expenses		
(phone, copying, fax, room rental, transcription, hospitality, local travel)		4,500
TOTAL FOCUS GROUPS		$20,900
Analysis and Strategy Development		
Principal	60	$ 4,500
GRAND TOTAL CHARGES		$46,250

PROPOSAL TO HILLTOP THEATER FOR CAPITAL CAMPAIGN FEASIBILITY STUDY AND CAMPAIGN PLAN

Introduction

At a time when most nonprofit performing arts organizations are adjusting to diminishing resources, Hilltop Theater has experienced remarkable growth and stabilization. After five years of successful operation at Hilltop's Theater Arts Center, they have opened a larger second stage in a rented facility.

With support for Hilltop (and visibility) high, the board and staff want to consider a modest capital campaign to allow purchase and further renovation of the downtown site.

Arts Consulting Associates proposes to assist Hilltop in assessing the feasibility of such a campaign at this time and—if warranted—developing an appropriate campaign action plan and timeline. What follows is a brief workplan, timeline, and budget for consulting services in connection with the feasibility study and campaign plan.

Workplan

I. Feasibility Study

It is common practice to conduct a feasibility study prior to preparing a capital campaign plan. This study, which looks outward at the context for the campaign as well as inward at the organization's own readiness, can help to set parameters for sensible, appropriate campaign planning.

A. Market Survey

The first task of the proposed feasbility study will be a market survey. Through a series of 24 to 30 in-depth interviews, we will develop a detailed picture of the constituents' views of Hilltop. We will interview donors, business, community and civic leaders, audience members, actors, volunteers, and staff using structured protocols prepared in advance. The second aspect of the market survey will include a review of secondary data that might establish external trends, obstacles, or opportunities which could positively or negatively affect Hilltop's proposed campaign. This data might include recent census information, regional periodicals, and data from the local Chambers of Commerce.

B. Organizational Assessment

This task will involve a careful examination of Hilltop's staffing and systems along with board and volunteer strengths and resources available to the campaign efforts. In this step we will interview board and staff and review basic documents such as budgets, fundraising and PR materials, donor files, and plans to determine Hilltop's readiness to launch a capital campaign.

C. Report Preparation/Presentation

We will summarize our findings in a comprehensive report with specific recommendations for enhancing Hilltop's readiness for a campaign. We will then present the report to the board and staff in a workshop setting to encourage discussion and action on the recommendations.

II. *Campaign Plan*

A. Develop Basic Campaign Structure and Solicitation Process

After full consideration of the feasibility study, it should be possible to develop the most sensible approach for Hilltop, considering all the circumstances. We will therefore work with a small campaign team to outline the structure of the campaign (i.e., detailing leadership and accountability) basic approaches to the campaign which are appropriate both to Hilltop's strengths and the circumstances (e.g., events, face-to-face, phone, mail, or a combination), and the overall process for solicitation. The work of this small team could then be presented to the full board for discussion, refinement, and approval.

B. Develop Basic Case Statement

With an outline of the campaign, we would once again work with the small team to outline and draft the key solicitation tool: the case statement. This most crucial of campaign documents should receive broad review by representatives of Hilltop's various constituencies to ensure that it is well crafted for its intended audiences.

C. Identify, Research, and Rate Prospects

This task will involve prospecting interviews with all Hilltop board (and some former board) members to identify and augment the theater's donor/prospect database. We will then work with the small campaign team to create a proposed "pyramid of giving" for discussion by the board.

D. Develop Campaign Support Materials

With a good understanding of campaign prospects, basic approaches and campaign structure, it should be possible to detail the types and quality of campaign support materials. Again, we will work with the Hilltop staff and campaign team to develop budgets, charts, graphs, brochure copy, and background materials appropriate to the tasks at hand.

E. Draft Action Plan and Timeline

A detailed action plan would then be drafted, identifying key campaign tasks and individuals responsible for each task. A timeline by task will be a critical campaign management tool.

F. Training

With all key campaign materials drafted, strategies, timing, and responsibilities outlined, it will be time to conduct a series of solicitor trainings. These half-day workshops will include coaching in "making the ask," practice in articulating key components of the campaign case statement, and role playing. Emphasis will be placed on teamwork in solicitation.

G. Follow-up

Subsequent to training, Hilltop's volunteer solicitors should be well prepared to begin the cultivation and solicitation process. We will follow up with the teams twice in the first quarter of campaign implementation to debrief with solicitors, provide analysis of preliminary responses, and adjust the campaign plan, if necessary.

PROPOSED TIMELINE

Hilltop Theater Capital Campaign Feasibility Study and Campaign Plan:
Proposed Timeline for Consultation

Task	June	July	Aug.	Sept.	Oct.	Nov.	Dec.	Jan.	Feb.	March
I. Feasibility Study										
A. Market Survey	XX	XXXX								
B. Organizational Assessment		XXXX								
C. Report			XX							
II. Campaign Plan										
A. Structure			XX							
B. Case Statement				XX						
C. Prospects				XX						
D. Materials					XXXX					
E. Timeline					XX	XX				
F. Training						XX	XX			
G. Follow-up								X		X

PROPOSED BUDGET

Hilltop Theater Capital Campaign Feasibility Study and Campaign Plan: Proposed Budget

Phase I - Feasibility Study

	# hours	charge		
A. Market Survey				
Lead Consultant	16	1,200		
Associate	32	1,440		
B. Organizational Assessment				
Lead Consultant	16	1,200		
Associate	20	900		
C. Report Preparation/Presentation				
Lead Consultant	16	1,200		
Associate	16	720		
SUBTOTAL FEES			6,660	
Clerical Support			400	
Travel				
mileage			330	
motel/meals			400	
Other Expenses				
(copying, phone, fax, postage)			250	
TOTAL — PHASE 1				8,040

PROPOSED BUDGET, continued

Hilltop Theater Capital Campaign Feasibility Study and Campaign Plan: Proposed Budget

Phase II - Feasibility Study

	# hours	charge		
A. Develop Basic Campaign Structure and Solicitation Process				
Lead Consultant	8	600		
Associate	24	1,080		
B. Develop Basic Case Statement				
Lead Consultant	8	600		
Associate	16	720		
C. Identify, Research, and Rate Prospects				
Lead Consultant	8	600		
Associate	16	720		
D. Develop Campaign Support Materials				
Lead Consultant	8	600		
Associate	24	1,080		
E. Draft Action Plan with Detailed Timeline				
Lead Consultant	8	600		
Associate	16	720		
F. Solicitor Training				
Lead Consultant	8	600		
Associate	8	360		
G. Follow-up				
Lead Consultant	8	600		
Associate	16	720		
SUBTOTAL FEES			9,600	
Clerical Support			600	
Travel				
mileage			330	
motel/meals			400	
Other Expenses				
(copying, phone, fax, postage)			350	
TOTAL — PHASE II				11,280
GRAND TOTAL				19,320

How Much Will a Consultant Cost – And When Do I Have To Pay?

Prices will vary wildly. Hourly rates can range from a rock-bottom fee of $35 per hour to ten times that amount. Many consultants will prefer to bid on the complete job, making it more difficult to determine what they're receiving per day unless you get a precise breakdown of their tasks and hours.

The relatively high fees charged by consultants (in a sector that notoriously underpays its employees) can cause some resentment within your organization. Discretion is the better part of fee negotiation. (And keep in mind that your consultant must pay his or her own overhead, health benefits, and insurance out of the fees.)

Parenthetically, sometimes the scope of the job will change – and you may decide to employ the consultant for additional duties. In these cases, you can always renegotiate the costs. But if the consultant underbids the original job, that's his or her problem – and you're under no obligation to make adjustments. The prudent consultant will bid fairly and complete the job within the constraints of the proposed budget.

The pay schedule can be worked out satisfactorily through one of three basic arrangements:

- *A periodic payment schedule* in which you agree to pay the consultant a fixed sum at regular intervals (probably monthly or quarterly) throughout the course of the project, presuming satisfactory progress.

- *A pay-as-you-go arrangement* in which you'll pay for each task or component of the project as it's completed.

- *A lump sum payment* due at the end of the project – probably of relatively short duration. (Consultants are less likely to agree to this kind of arrangement. Obviously, they run the risk of their fee going unpaid after completing an assignment.)

You should never agree to pay the consultant's full fee upfront, although payment of a retainer is common practice. The practice of working with fundraisers on a contingency basis is often criticized in the nonprofit sector. In fact, the National Society for Fund Raising Executives deems contingency work to be unethical and most seasoned professionals agree. The contingency arrangement *may* work well for you, but often it simply offers novice fundraisers without proven skills or a track record a route to break into the profession – and it can cause terrible public relations problems should the arrangement become known to your donors.

Contracts Without Lawyers

Good faith is the essence of the successful consulting relationship. One of the ways of maintaining the parameters of good faith is a written contract to formalize the terms of your arrangement. The contract is not a substitute for the workplan. Rather, the contract affirms the business aspects and financial parameters of the consulting relationship.

Your contract won't necessarily require a lawyer. It needn't run on for pages and contain confusing legalese. It's a document for clarification, meant to head off problems at the start.

The contract should contain:

- an acknowledgment of the workplan guiding the project.

- beginning and completion dates for the work.

- the fee.

- the exact date (or dates) when fee payments are due.

- any late charges for delinquent payments.

- termination procedures.

- the means of resolving disputes.

It is also advisable to build in "audit points" or times for you to sit down with your consultant and review progress to date before work continues. These meetings can help you refine your understanding of the process, or they can be an opportunity to head off trouble if things aren't exactly going as planned.

Following is a copy of a very simple contract for consulting services.

SAMPLE – CONTRACT FOR CONSULTING SERVICES

January 2, 1991

The Zoo Friends Association
John Lyon
123 Anywhere Street
San Francisco, CA 94102

Dear John:

This letter will serve as a confirmation of the contract between the Zoo Friends Association and Expert Consulting Firm (ECF) for a management survey and report with recommendations.

The scope of the work to be performed is described in our proposed workplan (copy attached). The contract amount is a total of $5,000.00. We anticipate working together through March 15th of 1991 in completing this survey and report. Our interim report on the project will be presented by February 15th.

We will submit our invoices on February 15th for half of the contract amount and a final invoice on March 15th with the delivery of the final report. Our invoices are due and payable upon receipt. If payment is not received within thirty days of the postmarked date of the invoice, a late fee of 1% of the invoice amount will be assessed for each month of nonpayment.

We here agree that any dispute arising out of this agreement will be submitted to binding arbitration in accordance with the laws of the state of California.

We acknowledge that either party retains the option to terminate this contract on thirty days written notice.

If you accept the terms set forth in this agreement, please sign in the space indicated below and return a copy to us. An additional copy is enclosed for your files.

We look forward to our work together on this project.

Sincerely,

Carla Consultant

Signed: _____ Date:_____
(for the Zoo Friends Association)

CONSULTANTS AT WORK

What they do – and how you can help (or hinder) the process

"To lead the people, walk behind them."

– Lao-Tzu

Modern management consulting got its start in late nineteenth-century America with an engineer from Germantown, Pennsylvania, named Frederick W. Taylor. Among other things, Taylor urged "a complete mental revolution" on the part of workers and managers that would result in a "scientifically" calibrated labor force leading to increased production. What he's usually remembered for is the storm of "time-and-motion studies" so often satirized in the movies by efficiency-crazed experts perched above the factory floor scribbling madly in their notebooks and clicking off production quotas on their stop watches.

Today's consultant, as we have seen, has blossomed, branched out, or overrun (depending on how you feel about consultants) Taylor's original area of expertise in favor of a more generalized approach to organizational change. Today, consultants, particularly in the nonprofit world, approach management problems with a nod to the organizational *gestalt* – the unified physical and psychological, as well as professional, configuration of the work experience. If that sounds daunting or pretentious, then let's just say that the contemporary consultant now looks at *and* beyond the specific task. A good financial consultant, for example, will not only keep an eye on the numbers, he or she will also be concerned with the bookkeeper's work space, the executive's supervisory style, and the organizational goals that the financial system is supposed to help track.

WHAT DOES THE CONSULTANT ACTUALLY DO?

It would be as exhausting to detail the precise methods applied by consultants to nonprofit problems as it would be to list the areas in which nonprofit groups work. The nonprofit sector is a vast, varied, complicated universe of social action and aspiration. Its concerns run the gamut from arts to zoos. Competent consultants vary their methods and strategies accordingly. That said, there is a predictable work routine that most consultants employ. While admitting that real life is much messier than workbook explanations (one stage of the consulting process often bleeds into another stage), we will break up this work routine into four parts: initial contact, assessment, action, and evaluation.

Initial Contact: Getting to Know You

Your relationship with the consultant begins with the interview. By the time the consultant has been hired, you'll each have some opinions about the other.

Your next step involves deepening your perception of the organizational problem. "While at work, a consultant is like a sponge," wrote Joseph Golden, "quickly absorbing a rich mixture of data, opinion, attitude, personalities and ideas. This mass of accumulated impressions – both literal and subjective – will have to undergo a complex processing, will demand time to digest, sort out, reorganize."

One of the consultant's most valuable attributes is his fresh eye on old troubles. In fact, your consultant should be able to take a long, hard look at the problems and potential that may have become invisible to you over time.

The good consultant will also fight hard to maintain his or her neutrality. If your organization has become divided over an issue or strategy, early in the relationship the consultant will want to meet with people from the opposing factions. The consultant will listen, encourage open discussion, collect information, but won't take sides. From the beginning, the conscientious consultant will probably shake things up. And almost certainly the consultant will make more work for you. But he or she should not exacerbate tensions or fuel disputes.

Assessment: What's Going Right and Wrong

As we've discussed, many nonprofit managers and boards feel overwhelmed by the variety and complexity of their organizational problems. Yet while they may not know how to solve these problems, they almost always have some instinctive feelings about the first steps that need to be taken.

Before coming to conclusions about the true cause of organizational distress, the consultant will often encourage staff and board to articulate these gut feelings. Sometimes the mere presence of the consultant-outsider will give people the opportunity, courage, or permission to express what everybody inside the organization already knows to be true. ("We need to fire the bookkeeper," "hire a bookkeeper," "change board leadership.") More often, these early interviews prepare people for a more extensive and challenging analysis of their organizational life.

The crux of the matter remains: How do you determine *what are the right questions* and then create an environment in which people's ideas, ambition, concerns, uncertainties, dread, and inspired dreams can all be given their due?

The short answer to this question is to flip to the section in Part III of this book, Six Self-Assessment Tools.

Part III contains a set of tools that can help any organization (with or without a consultant) pose the right questions and get useful responses.

Of course, your consultant may have his or her own tools. If so, you can use the tools in this workbook yourself to oversee the consulting process, making certain that the key questions and issues eventually get raised.

Action: Making Something Happen

Action simply refers to your *response* to organizational problems. And actions take time—overnight remedies seldom result in lasting change.

Common actions in collaboration with consultants include:

- *concrete tasks* such as installing a new computer or bookkeeping system.

- *problem solving between people* so that key staff and board can better communicate and cooperate in their work.

- *planning* for specific projects or long-term goals.

- *training* staff or board how to fundraise, supervise volunteers, or conduct other ongoing activities.

- *producing reports* that outline the feasibility of a future course—such as starting a capital campaign—or providing analyses of specific or general conditions within the organization.

Often the process of taking action—usually involving board and staff working together—will be one of the keys to remedying core conflicts among board and staff. But even the best planned action can present formidable challenges to your organization: You may involve your group in new ways of thought, collaboration, and debate not normally fostered by your organizational culture—and a whole new set of conflicts may arise.

For example, your consultant may move the focus of action away from key individuals, such as the executive or board president, in favor of newly formed working groups. Most often these groups will place greater emphasis upon values such as consensus, participatory management, and congruency between individual and organizational goals.

Many nonprofit organizations, despite protests to the contrary, don't embody these kinds of democratic values. Nonprofit groups are generally run like businesses and public agencies—from the top down. As elsewhere in life, people are primarily identified with their roles, titles, status, and visible accomplishments. The intervention of the consultant who encourages more democratic values may elicit some objections in your organization. This may be good for your group—or it may not. Consultants are often effective at changing organizational systems and structures; they're not so good at transforming personalities and values.

Yet the group action represents the dominant style of modern nonprofit consulting. From the beginning, you must be aware of the values that the consultant brings to the process as well as the values you and your organization operate with. The clear-headed rejection or modification of the consultant's values is always far better than unconscious sabotage.

Regardless of the actions undertaken with the consultant, concerns about confidentiality will also arise. More than almost anything, confidentiality is essential to maintaining the integrity of the consulting process. Like therapists, lawyers, and trusted friends, consultants should be valued for their discretion.

Evaluation: Sorting Out Success

Successful collaboration with a consultant depends on determining what you want to accomplish at the *beginning* of the relationship.

In other words, if you haven't decided where you want to go, you'll probably never get there... But setting your direction at the beginning of the process isn't as easy as it sounds. Nor is it simple to evaluate the performance of even the best consultants.

In the next section, we'll examine evaluation in some detail.

But for the moment, try to keep the following in mind:

- *Evaluation is a continuing process.* Quality must be tracked from the beginning of the consulting relationship, with sufficient opportunities allowed for adjusting the process when it runs off course. Your consultant should be available to discuss his progress with you during regularly scheduled meetings or on an ad hoc basis.

- *Interim reports are necessary.* Any project lasting more than eight weeks probably requires a brief, written progress report by the midway point. This report can serve as the basis for a more detailed discussion with the consultant during which you make certain that everybody involved is holding up his or her end of the job. The consultant shouldn't devote a great deal of time to writing the report (i.e., it shouldn't significantly increase the cost of the services). It's an informal document, serving as an indicator of the project's general health, making explicit much of what you've probably already seen or intuited, and en-

suring that the overall focus remains steady. The report will not cap or complete discussion on the project—but rather open it up.

- *Nothing turns out as planned.* The consulting process usually produces both delightful new information and unwelcome revelations. As a result, some changes in strategy may be necessary. But resist the temptation to respond to each layer of discovery with a new policy or revised work plan. Hold steady until you can grasp the whole picture.

WHEN THE CONSULTING RELATIONSHIP FAILS

Sometimes the consulting process simply falls flat—it doesn't work. The consultant or the client can be the culprit; there are many ways to ruin a promising relationship.

These are the chief danger signals that you should watch out for:

- *Deadlines are missed.* Reliability is crucial. If your collaborator lacks the time, skill, commitment, or interest to keep up his or her side of the bargain, then you're in deep trouble. Confront this issue directly. Treat deadline inconsistency in the same way you'd deal with it from a staff member. But first, of course, make certain that you've provided the consultant with all the information and resources that you had promised—and on time.

- *Communication is difficult.* You could be calling too often. (You may be developing an unhealthy dependency on the consultant.) Or, the consultant is overcommitted and can't keep up with his or her present tasks. Demand that you get the full attention you've contracted for—or end the relationship.

- *Constant changes in the work plan.* As the consultant's road map, the work plan may need to be renegotiated during your collaboration as new information is unearthed or as initial strategies prove ineffective. But it should not be in constant flux. Usually the client, rather than the consultant, will be guilty of tinkering too much with the work plan—often because of (probably unconscious) uncertainty about the desirability of change or a failure to stipulate (or comprehend) the project's objectives. Another variation on this counter-productive theme is the constant shifting of the consultant's contact person inside your organiza-tion. From the beginning, you should designate one person–probably the executive director or a board representative–to serve as the consult-ant's liaison. Otherwise, you can plan on dealing with immense confusion over roles, responsibili-ties, and the essential question of who is work-ing for whom.

- *Incessant emergencies.* Many consultants have learned to handle typical nonprofit emergencies with consummate skill and ease. Sometimes their interventions will be helpful and entirely appro-priate. (Who doesn't want the aid of a clever friend when the executive director suddenly quits, the bank closes your accounts, and the newspapers start talking scandal?) But be careful about developing an addiction to the momentary satisfactions of putting out *small* fires. The con-sulting process is most valuable in building long-term strength so that you can begin to anticipate and handle your own inevitable crises.

- *Overly ambitious plans.* Very often the organiza-tion seeking a consultant will hire somebody to help them with a specific area, such as fund development, only to be informed that their real problems lie in the area of planning or board development or some other related concern. These assessments are often correct. But they don't help much when payroll is due at the end of the month. It may be true that fundamental planning questions need to be answered (such as who are we and why do we exist?) before fund-raising can proceed. But it's also true that the group might have to launch into fundraising immediately, even before they're truly prepared, because they won't be able to continue operating without a quick infusion of cash. Obviously this isn't the best situation–but it's a common one. The concrete problems of daily management shouldn't be treated as though they're merely hypothetical situations safely contained within the consultant's notebook. Good consultants will

temper the ideal of an extensive, expansive, long-term relationship with the realities of his client's short-term needs.

- *The staff and board are at war.* Sometimes con-flict is necessary and unavoidable. But prolonged, unintended warfare will prove disastrous for any organization. This unhappy event may also in-dicate that your consultant does not grasp the complexities of group dynamics that can help you anticipate and prepare for the disputes. The consultant should be able to cool down con-flicts–or at least harness their energy to forge a new agenda for change. (That doesn't mean, of course, that your splintered organization will necessarily heed the call.) Ask yourself: What role are you playing in maintaining a system that isn't working?

- *Unrealistic predictions.* Unseasoned consultants may take a glance at your sloppy financial records and tell you to close up shop immediately. But you'll know better: Experience will have told you that things aren't perfect, but at least you've still got the commitment, energy, and resourceful-ness–along with the desire to learn the appro-priate skills–to continue the good fight. Other raw recruits to the consulting field may notice your organization's myriad problems, but fail to inform you about them for fear of alarming you and, thus, losing a client. Some people simply do not possess the flexibility and constitution to handle the climate of uncertainty inherent in the nonprofit structure. And despite their skill and good intentions, they will veer dangerously toward panic–or denial–and fail to provide you with real assistance.

The Last Word on Failure

In short, if the consulting process is going to break down, it's probably because of the same reasons that plague most other collaborations:

- unclear goals.

- unrealistic performance expectations.

- focus on the wrong problem.

- a loss of faith among collaborators.

- not enough time allocated to be truly effective.

- lack of honesty about the problems – and the difficulties in solving them.

Another possibility lies in the makeup of the organization itself. Some organizations simply won't change. They prefer the familiar, if uncomfortable strife that has given them definition and identity over the years. When the consultant has completed the job – delivering a plan for limited, specific improvements – he or she will find that the board and staff will not accept them.

Firing the Consultant

While firing somebody is never a pleasant task, the firing of a consultant should not present any special difficulties. Consultants live and die by their reputations;

they have everything to gain by making the termination as painless and private as possible. And even a simple contract can include provisions for termination.

On the other hand, you should be certain to report to your funder or any third party subsidizing or otherwise promoting your consultant why the relationship has ended prematurely. As we mentioned before, many groups prove reluctant to tell funders that their choice of consultant has been a failure. But that's the only way the field can be rid of incompetent consultants – or at least, consultants who've been poorly matched to a particular task.

You should also hold the consultant's last check until you receive your final report.

And now you're ready to stand back, wait, and determine whether it's all been worth the cost in money, time, and effort – as we'll see in the upcoming pages.

SEPARATION ANXIETY
Evaluating and concluding your consultant relationship

"Don't let your opinion sway your judgment."

— Sam Goldwyn

The consultant has now departed. What good did he or she actually do?

That's the tough question left facing you at the end of a long process that has absorbed much of your personal attention and many of your organizational dollars.

Very little research has been conducted to determine the specific types of consulting strategies that work best for nonprofit groups. It's no wonder researchers can't pinpoint the actions to be taken by consultants (who also differ in their professional goals, political opinions, organizational philosophies, and personalities) that will produce the same calculable effect on every nonprofit organization.

People have been searching for the formula to transform organizations since they've been building them. But *the* formula doesn't exist. Certain methods work at certain times with certain groups run by certain people.

The variables will always be with us.

HONEST EVALUATION:
LOOKING FOR MORE THAN A GOOD TIME

In truth, very few community-based groups have the time, money, inclination, or resources to construct a flawless evaluation process.

But there *are* concrete steps that any group can take to make certain that the evaluation retains its integrity and provides useful information.

To begin, keep in mind that *all good evaluations have a practical purpose.*

It makes sense to conduct a clear-eyed, comprehensive evaluation for the sake of your own organization. The consulting process has required a considerable in-

vestment of time and money. You must not skirt the inevitable question: Was it worth it—and under what circumstances should we do it again?

How Are Evaluations Conducted?

Most useful evaluations hinge upon two actions: the collection of data—followed by the data's analysis. In other words, what happened, and what does it mean?

Data collection is usually handled by engaging the key people in your project—those who implemented it and those affected by it—in filling out questionnaires, financial reports, and other tools for culling statistical and anecdotal information. These tools should be designed to track the project's original goals (clarified by you at the start of the consulting relationship) and measure the perceptions of the project's results. Obviously if your goals seemed fuzzy from the beginning, your evaluation will also be plagued by vagueness and uncertainty.

Once you've collected impressions and opinions, you'll need to organize the information—and then begin to puzzle out what it all means. This is where the critical matter of judgment comes to the fore.

To make the process work, you must be precise about which aspects of the project you want to evaluate.

A THOROUGH FOUR-PART EVALUATION

Rigorous evaluation demands that you step beyond the limited realm of subjective feelings. After all, evaluation aims for, well... *the truth.* And in order to track down this elusive quality, you'll need to separate the consulting process into four distinct, but related parts. These parts can then be judged independently in order to describe the overall quality of the entire consulting experience.

These are the aspects of the consulting relationship that you need to examine:

- *input*—your investment in the consulting relationship.

- *process*—your relationship with the consultant.

- *output*—the project.

- *outcomes*—your organization's progress towards its desired long-range goals.

Input: Your Investment in the Consulting Relationship

Your investment in your consultant and the consulting relationship goes beyond the fees you pay. It includes your commitment of time, information, cooperation, and more. When your work together is coming to a close, the first step in evaluation is to inventory how well you fulfilled your side of the bargain. Here are a few questions to help you with evaluating *your* input.

- Did your organization make a clear commitment to working with a consultant?

- Were your objectives clear and constant throughout the contract?

- Was the budget adequate?

- Did your consultant have access to the appropriate people in your organization?

- Did you provide thorough information in a timely manner?

- Did you offer feedback and clarification when appropriate?

Process: Your Relationship with the Consultant

While evaluations should not be popularity contests, it is important to check in with the people in your organization who worked most closely with the consultant. Their impressions and experiences will linger as time passes, shaping group attitudes about the value of consulting.

This part of the evaluation process isn't a human relations stunt meant to placate staff and draw attention to your own sensitivity as a manager. In truth, it will be helpful in making future organizational decisions about consulting to know:

- Did people *like* the consultant?

- Did they believe that the consultant helped them—and if so, in what ways?

- Did the consultant accomplish what he or she was hired to do?

- Was the work pace comfortable?

- Did the consultant appear to behave like a "professional"—was he or she on time, dressed appropriately, etc.?

- Did people feel that the consultant treated them with respect and consideration?

- Was the consultant flexible enough to adjust to his or her own changing perceptions of your organization and its problems—without losing sight of the project's original focus?

- Did the consultant provide any useful models of behavior, thought, or action that could be emulated by board or staff?

- Was communication improved among key people in your organization who worked with the consultant?

Of course, this level of evaluation will produce variations in response. And that's only natural; the expectations and personal interactions of your staff, board, and clients with the consultant will necessarily differ. Uniformity is not the goal. Rather, you'll be searching for a broad, generalized portrait of how the consultant affected people inside your organization, for good and ill.

Output: The Project

Unfortunately, many evaluations err on the side of good feelings and forget to ask this important question: Did the consultant do what was promised?

Fortunately you're on firmer ground in this area when there are specified, expected actions and products that can be measured. Among them, you should examine:

- the quantity and quality of your meetings with the consultant.

- the value of the consultant's work plan—and how closely it was followed during the project (or the appropriateness and necessity for any changes).

- the timeliness, accuracy, and usefulness of the consultant's reports.

- the long-term practicality of any new systems that the consultant may have introduced into your organization.

- whether the entire project, as described in the workplan, was completed in time and on budget.

This part of the evaluation should be relatively easy—*if* you've clarified your expectations in written form at the project's outset. But it's also at this stage that most evaluations usually stop—and that's too bad.

Outcomes: Progress Toward Long-Range Goals

After conscientiously examining the consultant's work in terms of process and production, many groups think that the evaluation has been concluded. But it's possible to have enormous personal affection for a smart and skilled consultant who has done exactly what was promised—and still not have a truly successful consulting relationship.

And that's because the *essential* question remains to be answered: Did the consultant's work help you to advance your organization's long-range goals?

It may take years to tell whether or not a specific intervention has pushed your organization further down the road to achieving its ultimate end. In fact, you may never know. But it's vital that you raise the question, because it delves to the heart of the most troublesome problem afflicting the nonprofit sector: the temptation to get caught up in the daily struggle for organizational survival, while failing to give sufficient attention to the fundamental reasons for existing.

It's easy to see how this happens. Most nonprofits tackle society's big problems: unemployment, hunger, housing, furthering education, culture, and art. Leaders of the very best organizations keep their eyes on a vision of broad social evolution; they're practical idealists, even as they slug it out daily in the trenches, making the small improvements that affect people in limited, but important ways.

By asking if the consultant has moved you along toward your primary goals, you'll be forced to examine the crucial issues that keep your organization honest about its aims and conscious of its potential. Unavoidably you'll find yourself asking the following:

- What are your goals?

- Are they shared by the staff and board?

- Do your work strategies help you to achieve your goals?

- Do you need to review, revise, and renew your statement of purpose because of new developments in the larger world beyond your office doors?

In the end, most successful consulting relationships will share a single goal: the institutionalization of organizational change. The best consultants promote new systems or ways of behaving that will help people in your organization to anticipate and solve problems as they arise in the future. The next section details a series of self-assessment tools that the nonprofit can adopt to effect change.

PART III

. . . .

Tools For Change

SIX SELF-ASSESSMENT TOOLS

How to identify the strengths and weaknesses of your governance, planning, fund development, financial management, public relations and marketing, and quality assurance

WORKING WITH THE TOOLS

The six self-assessment tools in Part III will help you to identify the strengths and weaknesses of your governance, planning, fund development, financial management, and public relations and marketing, as well as programs.

Whether they are working with a consultant or tackling the job alone, your entire board, staff, and possibly other significant people in your organizational family—such as deeply involved volunteers—should take part in the process. Drawn together, these people possess the greatest range and depth of knowledge about your organization. The tools will help them pinpoint your accomplishments and challenges for the future.

The tools may lead you quickly and easily to an obvious solution. (When you discover that your financial record keeping demands the skills of a bookkeeper, then you might consider hiring one.) Other times (or in other areas) the tools will encourage you to seek outside help in treating a specific problem area. (If you don't *have* any financial record keeping, then you may need a savvy advisor to help create the right systems for you.) In any case, the tools will serve as the *beginning* of a process that may take hours, days, weeks, or even months to complete. You can choose how quickly (or slowly) to proceed.

A few caveats are needed before the tools are actually picked up. Everybody using them should understand the following:

- *Personal opinions count.* Answer the questions from your own perspective within the organization. If you're a board member, then respond according to your focused interests, concerns, and responsibilities.

- *There is no single right answer.* These tools will assist you in describing the full range of knowledge and opinion regarding your organization and the variety (or lack) of expertise guiding its operations. Uncovering differences as well as areas of agreement will prove necessary in designing your approach to the future.

- *Time is on your side.* Each tool is purposefully divided into short sections so that self-assessment can be made a part of a series of board, committee, or staff meetings. On the other hand, you may wish to use a particular tool as the first step in addressing a crisis. For example, your board might use the governance tool to ferret out the root causes of flagging enthusiasm among its members.

- *"I don't know" is a perfectly respectable answer.* Don't be afraid to say it—it may point out an easily solvable problem.

Instructions for Use

It's easy. Here's how:

1. Decide which tool to try out first. Don't do everything at once. (If you're having a variety of problems, governance usually makes a good start.)

2. Determine exactly who will participate in the process of completing the self-assessment questionnaires. These tools were designed for

best results through "multiple-subjective assessment," which means at least three people participate and each holds a very different place in the organization (e.g., board member, executive staff and program staff, or volunteer).

3. Photocopy enough for everybody.

4. Distribute the tools with these instructions. You might even pass them out at your board and/or staff meetings. Set enough time aside to complete the forms.

5. Discuss the results immediately whenever possible, or collect the tools, compare the answers, and set aside the time for a thorough discussion of the results *in the near future*.

6. Once you've assessed an area of your operations, spend some creative time developing a range of possible actions or responses to the problem and test these ideas through discussion with other nonprofit board members or staff, with your consultant or other experts.

7. Get action. Initiate your solution(s), and carefully evaluate the outcomes.

GOVERNANCE

Basic legal requirements, the well-governed nonprofit organization, board effectiveness, executive leadership

INTRODUCTION

Every nonprofit organization is accountable for how it uses its funds and how it operates. The Federal, state, and sometimes even local governments routinely expect reports. In some states, the laws relating to the internal governance of nonprofit corporations are assembled in one place (a nonprofit Corporations Code). In others, the laws governing nonprofits are drawn from a variety of sources and depend heavily on analogies to for-profit corporations. Interpreting the laws and regulations that apply to nonprofits—or even finding them—may require persistence and a knowledgeable counselor. Nevertheless, ignorance of the law is never an excuse—nor is ignorance of your ignorance of the law.

This tool, in four parts, is meant to help you assess the strength and appropriateness of your organization's governance. The way we are using the term here, governance refers to oversight and policy making—the functions traditionally performed by an organization's board of directors in concert with executive staff. Management is addressed more directly in Part IV of this tool, which relates to executive leadership.

Governance: Basic legal requirements

Discussion

Part I of this tool is meant to help you see whether your organization is meeting the minimum legal requirements for keeping its privileged tax-exempt status. Some terms used may be unfamiliar to you. For example, this series of questions makes a reference to self-dealing by board members, a practice that is generally restricted. Most so-called self-dealing transactions are those where a board member stands to gain economically.

If your ability to answer any of the following questions is hampered by the appearance of unfamiliar terms, your first task in self-assessment is to define those terms.

Note: All board members share basic legal and financial responsibilities equally whether or not they are elected officers or committee chairs. The financial management tool is a good companion to this one.

1. Are your organization's programs clearly authorized by the statement of purpose in your Articles of Incorporation?

   ☐ Yes ☐ Needs Improvement ☐ No ☐ I don't know

2. Have your by-laws and Articles of Incorporation been reviewed recently enough to be sure of their appropriateness and compliance with current law?

   ☐ Yes ☐ Needs Improvement ☐ No ☐ I don't know

3. Is the board familiar with its basic legal responsibilities?

   ☐ Yes ☐ Needs Improvement ☐ No ☐ I don't know

4. Is the board familiar with the responsibilities it may NOT delegate to staff or committees according to law or your bylaws? (e.g., to fill board vacancies, amend or repeal by laws, fix director's compensation, etc.?)

   ☐ Yes ☐ Needs Improvement ☐ No ☐ I don't know

5. Are annual information returns filed with the Internal Revenue Service and appropriate state agencies in a timely manner each year?

   ☐ Yes ☐ Needs Improvement ☐ No ☐ I don't know

6. Is your organization complying with its responsibilities as an employer (e.g., withholdings, insurances, payroll taxes, and payroll tax returns)?

   ☐ Yes ☐ Needs Improvement ☐ No ☐ I don't know

7. Is surplus cash invested conservatively in line with fiduciary responsibilities?

   ☐ Yes ☐ Needs Improvement ☐ No ☐ I don't know

8. Do you have adequate insurance (e.g., disability, workers' comp, and general liability)?

   ☐ Yes ☐ Needs Improvement ☐ No ☐ I don't know

9. Are meeting and quorum requirements being observed as specified in your organization's bylaws?

   ☐ Yes ☐ Needs Improvement ☐ No ☐ I don't know

10. Are your organization's corporate records complete and up to date? (e.g., minutes, resolutions, financial reports?)

    ☐ Yes ☐ Needs Improvement ☐ No ☐ I don't know

11. Are you, as a board member, thoroughly familiar with the legal restrictions on self-dealing transactions?

    ☐ Yes ☐ Needs Improvement ☐ No ☐ I don't know

This tool was used by:

_____

(Name/title)   (date)

Governance:
The well-governed nonprofit organization

Discussion

We all know that doing the minimum is just that: the minimum. The following list of questions will help you set goals for excellence in governance (or perhaps to discover that your organization is already exceptional). The questions in this section are asking for *your* subjective feelings about your organization's governance. Financial management is a central part of good governance and an important component of planning. Please refer to those tools as well.

Note: A small, volunteer-based group less than three years old will almost undoubtedly *require* that board members serve many functions that would properly be the province of staff in an older, more established institution.

1. Does the board meet frequently enough to stay well informed and to participate in important policy decisions?

   ☐ Yes ☐ Needs Improvement ☐ No ☐ I don't know

2. Is the board the right size to provide for the governance of your organization?

   ☐ Yes ☐ Needs Improvement ☐ No ☐ I don't know

3. Do you have good attendance at board meetings?

   ☐ Yes ☐ Needs Improvement ☐ No ☐ I don't know

4. Do you have good participation at board meetings?

   ☐ Yes ☐ Needs Improvement ☐ No ☐ I don't know

5. Does your organization have a committee structure that makes sense?

   ☐ Yes ☐ Needs Improvement ☐ No ☐ I don't know

6. Are board and committee members generally prepared and qualified for the tasks they plan and undertake?

   ☐ Yes ☐ Needs Improvement ☐ No ☐ I don't know

7. Are committees effective?

   ☐ Yes ☐ Needs Improvement ☐ No ☐ I don't know

8. Is communication between board and staff adequate?

   ☐ Yes ☐ Needs Improvement ☐ No ☐ I don't know

9. Are board and staff both clear on the differences between their roles?

   ☐ Yes ☐ Needs Improvement ☐ No ☐ I don't know

10. Are board decisions communicated clearly within the board and to the staff when appropriate?

    ☐ Yes ☐ Needs Improvement ☐ No ☐ I don't know

11. Do board and staff work well together?

    ☐ Yes ☐ Needs Improvement ☐ No ☐ I don't know

12. Is conflict within your organization usually resolved in a constructive way?

    ☐ Yes ☐ Needs Improvement ☐ No ☐ I don't know

13. Do you have written personnel policies?

    ☐ Yes ☐ Needs Improvement ☐ No ☐ I don't know

14. Is there someone within your organization (or accessible to you) who is knowledgeable about the laws and regulations governing human resource management?

    ☐ Yes ☐ Needs Improvement ☐ No ☐ I don't know

15. Are staff and board morale good?

    ☐ Yes ☐ Needs Improvement ☐ No ☐ I don't know

16. Are people in key positions (e.g., executive director, development director, board chair, treasurer) well qualified to fulfill their roles?

    ☐ Yes ☐ Needs Improvement ☐ No ☐ I don't know

17. Is training made available for both board and staff when appropriate/needed?

    ☐ Yes ☐ Needs Improvement ☐ No ☐ I don't know

This tool was used by:

_____

(Name/title)   (date)

Governance: Board effectiveness

Discussion

To be effective, the board's role must be well defined, understood, and agreed to. Once defined, board members must also be prepared to fill those roles. This means that they must— individually and collectively— have skills, resources, commitment, and the time to share all of these with your organization.

Traditionally, boards of nonprofit agencies take responsibility for setting policy, planning for the organization's future, fundraising, financial management, and oversight of executive staff. They regularly offer expertise and function as ambassadors for the organization in the community.

The following brief list of questions was developed especially for board members.

You're a board member. At the outset you're committed enough to this organization and the cause it espouses to give of your time and expertise to help it achieve its goals. The following list of questions is meant to help you uncover opportunities for improving the effectiveness of your board as a team.

---

1. Do you know why you were asked to join the board?

   ☐ Yes ☐ Needs Improvement ☐ No ☐ I don't know

2. When you joined the board, were you adequately briefed about time and financial commitments?

   ☐ Yes ☐ Needs Improvement ☐ No ☐ I don't know

3. Do you feel your role (and the role of the board in general) is well enough defined?

   ☐ Yes ☐ Needs Improvement ☐ No ☐ I don't know

4. Do you feel you are well prepared to fulfill your role?

   ☐ Yes ☐ Needs Improvement ☐ No ☐ I don't know

5. Does your board work offer you a change from your everyday responsibilities?

   ☐ Yes ☐ Needs Improvement ☐ No ☐ I don't know

6. Is your board work satisfying?

   ☐ Yes ☐ Needs Improvement ☐ No ☐ I don't know

7. Are there currently enough active members on your board?

   ☐ Yes ☐ Needs Improvement ☐ No ☐ I don't know

8. Is your board regularly refreshed by the addition of new members?

   ☐ Yes ☐ Needs Improvement ☐ No ☐ I don't know

9. Is the racial, sexual, and cultural composition of your board appropriate to your constituency and your mission as well as the tasks you must carry out?

   ☐ Yes ☐ Needs Improvement ☐ No ☐ I don't know

10. Are you offered training from time to time?

    ☐ Yes ☐ Needs Improvement ☐ No ☐ I don't know

11. Do you feel you have enough information about your organization's day-to-day operations to make decisions concerning them?

    ☐ Yes ☐ Needs Improvement ☐ No ☐ I don't know

12. Do you generally feel satisfied by board meetings?

    ☐ Yes ☐ Needs Improvement ☐ No ☐ I don't know

This tool was used by:

_____

(Name/title)   (date)

Governance: Executive leadership

Discussion

You might say that leadership is to governance what fuel is to a car. But the *kind* of leadership a nonprofit organization needs will change as the organization itself changes in response to environmental conditions and policy decisions. Good leadership may be the result of talent or experience, but most often it is an interesting combination of head and heart, experience, *and* intuition. An outstanding leader in the for-profit as well as the nonprofit sector has a broad repertoire of possible responses to problems. Some responses will be logical, some will be instinctual, and the gifted leader shifts readily from one strategy to another as he or she assesses an organization's needs on an ongoing basis.

The following series of questions is divided into two interchangeable parts: The first is a series specifically designed for board members to help them assess the effectiveness of the organization's executive *and* of their own role in nurturing leadership in their executive. The second, and directly parallel series, is drafted specifically for executive directors so that they

may participate fully in this diagnosis.

In using this tool, you will find many levels of inquiry. Some questions relate directly to executive director preparedness for the role in terms of skills, knowledge, and commitment. Other questions delve into the areas of communication, role definition, and expectations. Still others focus on the essential ingredient of mutual support among all levels of an organization.

More detailed focus is given to planning and research concerns in the planning and quality assurance tools, respectively.

As with all the other tools in this series, sharing the results and taking the time to discuss them together is the first–and also a lasting–benefit of the process.

Note: As with all the tools in this chapter, remember–they were not designed to "test" or to be used as a weapon. Approach this next series of questions as you would a road map when stopping part way on a long trip. Take the opportunity to note how far you've come as well as the distance (and tricky curves) ahead. Then, get on with it.

A. For Executive Directors

1. Do you feel you have a complete understanding of the mission of your organization?

   ☐ Yes ☐ Needs Improvement ☐ No ☐ I don't know

2. Are you confident in your ability to articulate the mission and to excite others about it?

   ☐ Yes ☐ Needs Improvement ☐ No ☐ I don't know

3. Are you a capable communicator in general? Are you able to articulate a vision of your organization's future?

   ☐ Yes ☐ Needs Improvement ☐ No ☐ I don't know

4. Do you feel you possess the right mix of experience, skill, understanding, and commitment?

   ☐ Yes ☐ Needs Improvement ☐ No ☐ I don't know

5. In your estimation, have you proven your ability to see that the mission is carried forward?

   ☐ Yes ☐ Needs Improvement ☐ No ☐ I don't know

6. Do you know enough about the environmental factors that affect your organization (community, political context, laws and regulations, funding opportunities, etc.)?

   ☐ Yes ☐ Needs Improvement ☐ No ☐ I don't know

7. Are you well aware of your organization's history and how it fits in the community?

   ☐ Yes ☐ Needs Improvement ☐ No ☐ I don't know

8. Do you have a good sense of how other service providers perceive your organization?

   ☐ Yes ☐ Needs Improvement ☐ No ☐ I don't know

9. Do you adequately understand current and potential "markets" for your organization's programs and services?

☐ Yes ☐ Needs Improvement ☐ No ☐ I don't know

10. Do you manage the growing/changing needs of your organization effectively?

☐ Yes ☐ Needs Improvement ☐ No ☐ I don't know

11. In general, does the board have a clear idea of what your job responsibilities are?

☐ Yes ☐ Needs Improvement ☐ No ☐ I don't know

12. Do you fully understand what the board expects of you?

☐ Yes ☐ Needs Improvement ☐ No ☐ I don't know

13. Do you feel your skills are well matched to your job responsibilities?

☐ Yes ☐ Needs Improvement ☐ No ☐ I don't know

14. In general, are the board's expectations of you reasonable in light of available resources (e.g., time, money, support staff)?

☐ Yes ☐ Needs Improvement ☐ No ☐ I don't know

15. Are you capable of making difficult decisions when required?

☐ Yes ☐ Needs Improvement ☐ No ☐ I don't know

16. Are you able to set priorities?

☐ Yes ☐ Needs Improvement ☐ No ☐ I don't know

17. Do you follow through on tasks?

☐ Yes ☐ Needs Improvement ☐ No ☐ I don't know

18. Do you recognize and acknowledge when you need outside assistance, counsel, or training?

☐ Yes ☐ Needs Improvement ☐ No ☐ I don't know

19. Have you proven to be capable of motivating the organization's staff?

☐ Yes ☐ Needs Improvement ☐ No ☐ I don't know

20. Are you capable of helping the staff with their professional development?

☐ Yes ☐ Needs Improvement ☐ No ☐ I don't know

21. Are you able to adequately supervise and work with consultants and other outside experts?

☐ Yes ☐ Needs Improvement ☐ No ☐ I don't know

22. Are you appropriately involved in board development?

☐ Yes ☐ Needs Improvement ☐ No ☐ I don't know

23. Do you communicate effectively and frequently enough with the board of directors?

☐ Yes ☐ Needs Improvement ☐ No ☐ I don't know

24. Are you risking burnout (e.g., feeling frustrated or angry too often)?

☐ Yes ☐ Needs Improvement ☐ No ☐ I don't know

25. Are you in communication with other executives in the field (sufficient to feel connected to and supported by your colleagues)?

☐ Yes ☐ Needs Improvement ☐ No ☐ I don't know

26. Do you help the staff avoid burnout?

☐ Yes ☐ Needs Improvement ☐ No ☐ I don't know

27. Do you create adequate opportunities for board and staff interaction?

☐ Yes ☐ Needs Improvement ☐ No ☐ I don't know

28. Do you function effectively as an advocate internally in your organization (staff to board and board to staff)?

☐ Yes ☐ Needs Improvement ☐ No ☐ I don't know

29. Do you feel you serve as a positive role model for staff?

☐ Yes ☐ Needs Improvement ☐ No ☐ I don't know

30. Is the board president accessible enough to you and your staff?

    ☐ Yes ☐ Needs Improvement ☐ No ☐ I don't know

31. Does your board president put enough time in to be an effective partner in leading your organization?

    ☐ Yes ☐ Needs Improvement ☐ No ☐ I don't know

32. Do you feel that you and your board president fully understand and support each other in your respective roles?

    ☐ Yes ☐ Needs Improvement ☐ No ☐ I don't know

33. Does the board work closely with you in recruiting and training new board members?

    ☐ Yes ☐ Needs Improvement ☐ No ☐ I don't know

34. Do you have enough "room" and independence to carry out the mission efficiently?

    ☐ Yes ☐ Needs Improvement ☐ No ☐ I don't know

35. Do you have enough challenges in your job?

    ☐ Yes ☐ Needs Improvement ☐ No ☐ I don't know

36. In general, does the board have a healthy level of confidence in your ability to direct the organization?

    ☐ Yes ☐ Needs Improvement ☐ No ☐ I don't know

37. Is your work sufficiently acknowledged and appreciated by the board and your coworkers?

    ☐ Yes ☐ Needs Improvement ☐ No ☐ I don't know

38. Are you appropriately involved in planning for your organization's future?

    ☐ Yes ☐ Needs Improvement ☐ No ☐ I don't know

39. Are you fairly and regularly evaluated by the board?

    ☐ Yes ☐ Needs Improvement ☐ No ☐ I don't know

40. Are criteria for your evaluation agreed upon in advance?

    ☐ Yes ☐ Needs Improvement ☐ No ☐ I don't know

41. Are these criteria concrete enough?

    ☐ Yes ☐ Needs Improvement ☐ No ☐ I don't know

42. Are they tied closely to the organization's long-range goals and objectives?

    ☐ Yes ☐ Needs Improvement ☐ No ☐ I don't know

43. Does the board nurture you in your own professional development?

    ☐ Yes ☐ Needs Improvement ☐ No ☐ I don't know

This tool was used by:

_____

(Name/title)   (date)

B. For Board Members

1. Do you feel your executive director has a complete understanding of the mission of your organization?

   ☐ Yes ☐ Needs Improvement ☐ No ☐ I don't know

2. Are you confident in the executive director's ability to articulate the mission and to excite others about it?

   ☐ Yes ☐ Needs Improvement ☐ No ☐ I don't know

3. Is the executive director a capable communicator in general? Is he or she able to articulate a vision of your organization's future?

   ☐ Yes ☐ Needs Improvement ☐ No ☐ I don't know

4. Do you feel your executive director possesses the right mix of experience, skill, understanding, and commitment?

   ☐ Yes ☐ Needs Improvement ☐ No ☐ I don't know

5. In your estimation, has he or she proven the ability to see that the mission is carried forward?

   ☐ Yes ☐ Needs Improvement ☐ No ☐ I don't know

6. Does your executive director knows enough about the environmental factors that affect your organization (community, political context, laws and regulations, funding opportunities, etc.)?

   ☐ Yes ☐ Needs Improvement ☐ No ☐ I don't know

7. Is he or she well aware of your organization's history and how it fits in the community?

   ☐ Yes ☐ Needs Improvement ☐ No ☐ I don't know

8. Does the executive director have a good sense of how other service providers perceive your organization?

   ☐ Yes ☐ Needs Improvement ☐ No ☐ I don't know

9. Does he or she adequately understand current and potential "markets" for your organization's programs and services?

   ☐ Yes ☐ Needs Improvement ☐ No ☐ I don't know

10. Does he or she manage the growing/changing needs of your organization adequately?

    ☐ Yes ☐ Needs Improvement ☐ No ☐ I don't know

11. In general, does the board have a clear idea of what the executive director's job responsibilities are?

    ☐ Yes ☐ Needs Improvement ☐ No ☐ I don't know

12. Does he or she fully understand what the board expects of him or her?

    ☐ Yes ☐ Needs Improvement ☐ No ☐ I don't know

13. Do you feel the executive director's skills are well matched to his or her job responsibilities?

    ☐ Yes ☐ Needs Improvement ☐ No ☐ I don't know

14. In general, are the board's expectations of the executive director reasonable in light of available resources (e.g., time, money, support staff)?

    ☐ Yes ☐ Needs Improvement ☐ No ☐ I don't know

15. Is he or she capable of making difficult decisions when required?

    ☐ Yes ☐ Needs Improvement ☐ No ☐ I don't know

16. Is he or she able to set priorities?

    ☐ Yes ☐ Needs Improvement ☐ No ☐ I don't know

17. Does he or she follow through on tasks?

    ☐ Yes ☐ Needs Improvement ☐ No ☐ I don't know

18. Does he or she recognize and acknowledge when she needs outside assistance, counsel or training?

    ☐ Yes ☐ Needs Improvement ☐ No ☐ I don't know

19. Has your executive director proven to be capable of motivating the organization's staff?

    ☐ Yes ☐ Needs Improvement ☐ No ☐ I don't know

20. Is he or she capable of helping the staff with their professional development?

    ☐ Yes ☐ Needs Improvement ☐ No ☐ I don't know

21. Is he or she able to adequately supervise and work with consultants and other outside experts?

    ☐ Yes ☐ Needs Improvement ☐ No ☐ I don't know

22. Is your executive director appropriately involved in board development?

    ☐ Yes ☐ Needs Improvement ☐ No ☐ I don't know

23. Does he or she communicate effectively and frequently enough with the board of directors?

    ☐ Yes ☐ Needs Improvement ☐ No ☐ I don't know

24. Do you feel he or she is risking burnout (e.g., appearing angry or frustrated too often)?

    ☐ Yes ☐ Needs Improvement ☐ No ☐ I don't know

25. Is your executive director in communication with other executives in the field (sufficient to feel connected to and supported by his or her colleagues)?

    ☐ Yes ☐ Needs Improvement ☐ No ☐ I don't know

26. Does he or she help the staff avoid burnout?

    ☐ Yes ☐ Needs Improvement ☐ No ☐ I don't know

27. Does he or she create adequate opportunities for board and staff interaction?

    ☐ Yes ☐ Needs Improvement ☐ No ☐ I don't know

28. Is your executive director functioning effectively as an advocate internally in your organization (staff to board, and board to staff)?

    ☐ Yes ☐ Needs Improvement ☐ No ☐ I don't know

29. Do you feel he or she serves as a positive role model for staff?

    ☐ Yes ☐ Needs Improvement ☐ No ☐ I don't know

30. Is the board president accessible enough to your executive director and his or her staff?

    ☐ Yes ☐ Needs Improvement ☐ No ☐ I don't know

31. Does your board president put enough time in to be an effective partner in leading your organization?

    ☐ Yes ☐ Needs Improvement ☐ No ☐ I don't know

32. Do you feel that your executive director and your board president fully understand and support each other in their respective roles?

    ☐ Yes ☐ Needs Improvement ☐ No ☐ I don't know

33. Does the board work closely with the executive director in recruiting and training new board members?

    ☐ Yes ☐ Needs Improvement ☐ No ☐ I don't know

34. Does the executive director have enough "room" and independence to carry out the mission efficiently?

    ☐ Yes ☐ Needs Improvement ☐ No ☐ I don't know

35. Does he or she have enough challenges in the job?

    ☐ Yes ☐ Needs Improvement ☐ No ☐ I don't know

36. In general, does the board have a healthy level of confidence in the executive director's ability to direct the organization?

    ☐ Yes ☐ Needs Improvement ☐ No ☐ I don't know

37. Is the executive director's work sufficiently acknowledged and appreciated by the board and his or her coworkers?

    ☐ Yes ☐ Needs Improvement ☐ No ☐ I don't know

38. Is he or she appropriately involved in planning for your organization's future?

    ☐ Yes ☐ Needs Improvement ☐ No ☐ I don't know

39. Is your executive director fairly and regularly evaluated by the board?

    ☐ Yes ☐ Needs Improvement ☐ No ☐ I don't know

40. Are criteria for his or her evaluation agreed upon in advance?

    ☐ Yes ☐ Needs Improvement ☐ No ☐ I don't know

41. Are these criteria concrete enough?

☐ Yes ☐ Needs Improvement ☐ No ☐ I don't know

42. Are they tied closely to the organization's long-range goals and objectives?

☐ Yes ☐ Needs Improvement ☐ No ☐ I don't know

43. Do you nurture the executive director in his or her own professional development?

☐ Yes ☐ Needs Improvement ☐ No ☐ I don't know

This tool was used by:

_____

(Name/title)   (date)

PLANNING

Setting a context, exploring your vision, the planning process

INTRODUCTION

Simply stated, planning is looking at the future and trying to design a feasible and appropriate approach to it. One popular way of *doing* planning for nonprofits is to examine issues, set goals and objectives, and then to design strategies for meeting them. Although objectives (time-phased, measurable outcomes) can be helpful in measuring progress toward a goal, there are other ways to think about the future of your organization constructively. Particularly with small, emerging organizations, "intuitive" planning is more the norm than formal strategic planning, which often results in long documents.

However, there is no substitute for a clear sense of purpose. There must be an awareness and commitment to the organization's mission (another word for purpose) that board and staff use to direct their policymaking and actions.

Note: No tool or plan will ensure your success. Relationships within the organization must be strong and based on mutual respect (board to staff and vice versa). The single most important relationship is between the executive director and board chairperson. Nurture it.

Planning: Setting a context

Discussion

Things are changing all the time. For example, government budget cuts may affect your organization's ability to serve an ever-increasing need. Or the growth of a new industry may result in greater prosperity (and more school-aged children) in your community. Comprehensive, up-to-date information about shifts and trends affecting your constituent groups can make the difference between an unrealistic, overly ambitious plan and a plan that helps your organization greet the future with confidence.

In fact, with increased competition for funding, the question of an organization's continued relevance is a proper area for active, periodic questioning. The following questions are meant to help you discover gaps in your organization's understanding of the external need your organization is working to fill. The second part of this tool will help you assess your organization's internal ability to meet that need. The third and final part of this tool is an exploration of the planning process itself.

Note: Quality assurance is an essential part of planning and good governance. We refer you to the final tool in our series for more details about evaluating your organization's performance.

---

1. Do you feel you know enough about your clients and constituents?

   ☐ Yes ☐ Needs Improvement ☐ No ☐ I don't know

2. Do you understand their needs and how your programs address those needs?

   ☐ Yes ☐ Needs Improvement ☐ No ☐ I don't know

3. Have you compared the characteristics of those you want to serve with those you actually serve?

   ☐ Yes ☐ Needs Improvement ☐ No ☐ I don't know

4. Are you aware of trends in your community (e.g., population shifts, economic changes etc.) that may affect your organization and the need for its programs?

   ☐ Yes ☐ Needs Improvement ☐ No ☐ I don't know

5. Do you understand the interrelationship of agencies in your region which provide similar services?

   ☐ Yes ☐ Needs Improvement ☐ No ☐ I don't know

6. Where you are competing (providing similar services to the same population as other organizations)? Are you doing it effectively?

   ☐ Yes ☐ Needs Improvement ☐ No ☐ I don't know

7. Do you regularly get outside input in planning and evaluating your programs?

   ☐ Yes ☐ Needs Improvement ☐ No ☐ I don't know

8. Do you evaluate your programs regularly against pre-established standards?

   ☐ Yes ☐ Needs Improvement ☐ No ☐ I don't know

This tool was used by:

_____

(Name/title)   (date)

Planning: Exploring your vision

Discussion

A good plan still may not paint an accurate picture of the future. (Who can?) But it *should* offer guidelines for operating, and it should also help in evaluating the success of your efforts. To work well for your organization, a plan need be neither a long document nor should it simply be carried around in someone's head.

The following questions are meant to help you discover whether or not the policymakers and implementors in your organization hold the same vision of the organization's purpose and the roads to take in pursuit of it.

---

1. Do you have a clear written statement of purpose for your organization?

   ☐ Yes ☐ Needs Improvement ☐ No ☐ I don't know

2. Does your statement of purpose adequately describe what your organization actually *does*?

   ☐ Yes ☐ Needs Improvement ☐ No ☐ I don't know

3. Do you agree that the statement of purpose reflects the current needs of the constituencies you serve?

   ☐ Yes ☐ Needs Improvement ☐ No ☐ I don't know

4. Is there general agreement that your organization is doing what it should be doing?

   ☐ Yes ☐ Needs Improvement ☐ No ☐ I don't know

5. Is your organization's direction (goals and plans) clear and understood?

   ☐ Yes ☐ Needs Improvement ☐ No ☐ I don't know

6. In general, does your organization achieve what is sets out to do?

   ☐ Yes ☐ Needs Improvement ☐ No ☐ I don't know

7. Are the skills needed to accomplish the organization's objectives accessible and being utilized?

   ☐ Yes ☐ Needs Improvement ☐ No ☐ I don't know

This tool was used by:

_____

(Name/title)   (date)

Planning: The planning process

Discussion

The following short series of questions outlines a basic strategic planning process—and one the authors have found to be effective with both emerging and midsized nonprofits. It begins with assessment and ends with job descriptions and budgets. And it's meant to echo much of what the other tools in this part point to.

---

1. Is there general agreement throughout your organization about the need to plan?

   ☐ Yes ☐ Needs Improvement ☐ No ☐ I don't know

2. Is there a common definition of basic planning terms within your organization (e.g., mission, goal, objective, strategy, stakeholder)?

   ☐ Yes ☐ Needs Improvement ☐ No ☐ I don't know

3. Are you willing and able to commit enough time to planning to ensure a good process and a quality product?

   ☐ Yes ☐ Needs Improvement ☐ No ☐ I don't know

4. Are you and your fellow planners actively seeking advice and impressions from throughout the organization as you plan?

   ☐ Yes ☐ Needs Improvement ☐ No ☐ I don't know

5. Will those who have responsibility for implementing the plan also have meaningful input into the planning process?

   ☐ Yes ☐ Needs Improvement ☐ No ☐ I don't know

6. Do you feel adequately prepared to plan effectively (i.e., well informed about your organization's accomplishments and challenges)?

   ☐ Yes ☐ Needs Improvement ☐ No ☐ I don't know

7. Have you explored the advantages of an outside facilitator to assist you with your planning meetings or retreats?

   ☐ Yes ☐ Needs Improvement ☐ No ☐ I don't know

8. Have you fully assessed your organization's strengths and weaknesses as a prelude to setting goals and objectives?

   ☐ Yes ☐ Needs Improvement ☐ No ☐ I don't know

9. Are you aware of the major commitments your organization has made that will structure (or limit) plans for the future?

   ☐ Yes ☐ Needs Improvement ☐ No ☐ I don't know

10. Is budget preparation an integral part of your planning process?

    ☐ Yes ☐ Needs Improvement ☐ No ☐ I don't know

11. Are you able to set clear priorities?

    ☐ Yes ☐ Needs Improvement ☐ No ☐ I don't know

12. Is responsibility for advancing plans clearly assigned?

    ☐ Yes ☐ Needs Improvement ☐ No ☐ I don't know

13. If you have a formal long-range plan, do you refer to it and revise it often enough?

    ☐ Yes ☐ Needs Improvement ☐ No ☐ I don't know

14. Do you feel you are planning too much?

    ☐ Yes ☐ Needs Improvement ☐ No ☐ I don't know

This tool was used by:

_____

(Name/title)   (date)

FUND DEVELOPMENT
General, individuals, grants, direct mail, events, special campaigns

INTRODUCTION

No organization can accomplish its goals without resources – facilities, equipment, time, and, of course, money.

Money won't cure your organizational ills, but a healthy organization – one that is clear about its mission, pays reasonable attention to planning, and has skilled management – still needs money to run programs (even if its main program is coordinating volunteers).

Each nonprofit organization has its own personality and capabilities. Fundraising plans should be sensitive to that personality (e.g., discover your strengths and play to them). New skills in fundraising can be acquired, and training is always a good option if your fundraising plans are limited by your existing capabilities.

This tool has six parts: *General, Individuals* (face-to-face), *Grants* (Foundations, Corporations, Government), *Direct Mail, Events,* and *Special Campaigns.*

Note: Successful fund development is almost always the result of teamwork and should be well coordinated with public relations and program plans.

Fund development: General

1. Do you have a written, annual fundraising plan?

   ☐ Yes   ☐ Needs Improvement   ☐ No   ☐ I don't know

2. Do you understand the difference between operating, capital, and endowment funds?

   ☐ Yes   ☐ Needs Improvement   ☐ No   ☐ I don't know

3. Do you understand the differences in fundraising for each?

   ☐ Yes   ☐ Needs Improvement   ☐ No   ☐ I don't know

4. Keeping past achievements and current capabilities in mind, do you set fundraising goals realistically?

   ☐ Yes   ☐ Needs Improvement   ☐ No   ☐ I don't know

5. Are most of your board members actively involved in some aspect of fund development?

   ☐ Yes   ☐ Needs Improvement   ☐ No   ☐ I don't know

6. Does your organization receive support from many (and diverse) sources?

   ☐ Yes   ☐ Needs Improvement   ☐ No   ☐ I don't know

7. Have you developed strategies for relating to "major donors"?

   ☐ Yes   ☐ Needs Improvement   ☐ No   ☐ I don't know

8. Are your executive and development staff well prepared to manage the planned fundraising campaigns??

   ☐ Yes   ☐ Needs Improvement   ☐ No   ☐ I don't know

9. Does your budget provide adequate resources (money and staff) to accomplish your fundraising objectives?

   ☐ Yes   ☐ Needs Improvement   ☐ No   ☐ I don't know

10. Do you–generally–achieve your fundraising goals?

    ☐ Yes   ☐ Needs Improvement   ☐ No   ☐ I don't know

11. Do you evaluate each fundraising campaign?

    ☐ Yes   ☐ Needs Improvement   ☐ No   ☐ I don't know

This tool was used by:

_____

(Name/title)   (date)

Fund development: Individuals

Discussion

Face-to-face, peer-to-peer fundraising is both the most effective way to raise funds and the most personally demanding. Few beginners are comfortable with simply asking their friends and colleagues for money. A successful individual fund drive depends on the confidence and comfort of the solicitors and on the quality of information available on potential individual donors.

Note: Volunteer solicitors, especially good ones, are in limited supply. Support them in their efforts and treat them well.

1. Do you have comprehensive, up-to-date information about your current donors? (e.g., their giving history, professional and civic activities, relationship to your organization?

   ☐ Yes ☐ Needs Improvement ☐ No ☐ I don't know

2. Do you do ongoing research to identify new prospects?

   ☐ Yes ☐ Needs Improvement ☐ No ☐ I don't know

3. Do you know how to do donor research?

   ☐ Yes ☐ Needs Improvement ☐ No ☐ I don't know

4. Is the dollar amount to be raised from individuals reasonable given your past achievements and current capabilities?

   ☐ Yes ☐ Needs Improvement ☐ No ☐ I don't know

5. Do you communicate with your donors regularly?

   ☐ Yes ☐ Needs Improvement ☐ No ☐ I don't know

6. Do you request renewal and/or upgraded gifts regularly (every 12 months)?

   ☐ Yes ☐ Needs Improvement ☐ No ☐ I don't know

7. Is your base of individual donors growing in numbers?

   ☐ Yes ☐ Needs Improvement ☐ No ☐ I don't know

8. Is the average size of gift from your individual donors growing?

   ☐ Yes ☐ Needs Improvement ☐ No ☐ I don't know

9. Do you know whether or not you are keeping a strong core of donors who renew their gifts from year to year?

   ☐ Yes ☐ Needs Improvement ☐ No ☐ I don't know

This tool was used by:

_____

(Name/title)   (Date)

Fund development: Grants

Discussion

Foundations, corporations, and government agencies with established giving programs almost always have guidelines for soliciting support. These guidelines—and priorities for giving—are as diverse as the founders and managers of the grant programs. There is no sub- stitute for up-to-date thorough research in this area.

Note: Grant writing and research about funders is usually a staff function. Board members may often appropriately answer "I don't know" to many of the questions in this section.

Foundations and Government

1. Do you know the funding priorities of the foundations in your region?

   ☐ Yes ☐ Needs Improvement ☐ No ☐ I don't know

2. Do you know the funding priorities of relevant state, local, and federal government agencies?

   ☐ Yes ☐ Needs Improvement ☐ No ☐ I don't know

3. Do you do regular research to identify new foundation and government prospects?

   ☐ Yes ☐ Needs Improvement ☐ No ☐ I don't know

4. Do your files include current annual reports and guidelines from all your current and potential foundation and government funders?

   ☐ Yes ☐ Needs Improvement ☐ No ☐ I don't know

5. Do you make timely, complete applications to the foundation and government agencies that you consider to be good prospects for funding your organization?

   ☐ Yes ☐ Needs Improvement ☐ No ☐ I don't know

6. Do you know the managers/program officers at the foundations and government agencies that fund your organization?

   ☐ Yes ☐ Needs Improvement ☐ No ☐ I don't know

7. Do you make timely, complete reports to funders?

   ☐ Yes ☐ Needs Improvement ☐ No ☐ I don't know

8. Do you exchange information about funders with other nonprofit organizations?

   ☐ Yes ☐ Needs Improvement ☐ No ☐ I don't know

Corporations

1. Are you well acquainted with the business leaders in your community?

   ☐ Yes ☐ Needs Improvement ☐ No ☐ I don't know

2. Can you offer a service to a corporation's employees (e.g., a corporate meeting place, employee assistance programs, etc.)?

   ☐ Yes ☐ Needs Improvement ☐ No ☐ I don't know

3. Can you/do you offer businesses visibility in connection with funding or sponsoring a project for your organization?

   ☐ Yes ☐ Needs Improvement ☐ No ☐ I don't know

4. Do you know which corporations in your community have gift matching programs?

   ☐ Yes ☐ Needs Improvement ☐ No ☐ I don't know

5. Does your board include representation from the business community?

   ☐ Yes ☐ Needs Improvement ☐ No ☐ I don't know

6. Do your regularly invite input from the business community?

   ☐ Yes ☐ Needs Improvement ☐ No ☐ I don't know

This tool was used by:

_____

(Name/title)   (Date)

Fund development: Direct mail

Discussion

It's axiomatic that personal solicitation by volunteers (peer-to-peer, face-to-face) is the most effective way to raise money. It is less well known, however, that direct mail is the next best strategy. But direct mail will not be cost-effective for every nonprofit.

Therefore, we have designed two series of questions. The first series is meant to help you decide whether or not direct mail is a good strategy for your organization in prospecting for and cultivating potential donors. If you're already involved in soliciting contributions through the mail, the second series should help you discover if you're making the most of the direct mail solicitation you're doing. Prospecting through the mail (e.g., looking for new donors) is expensive and requires a relatively large mailing list. Most experts begin with test mailings of 30,000 pieces or more.

Note: Direct mail is approached most often as a way to raise money, but it is also a powerful way to educate and inform. Well-coordinated direct mail campaigns may also help interest volunteers, attract renewable gifts or lay the groundwork for planned giving. A direct mail package presents a public image of your organization. In your efforts to make the mail a cost-effective way to generate contributions, pay close attention to what the "look" says. People don't give simply because your organization needs the money. They give for the same reasons you do: They are affected or impressed by the cause and the organization. Give them good reason to be!

Is Direct Mail For Your Organization?

1. Is your organization well known and well respected in the community where you will solicit?

   ☐ Yes ☐ Needs Improvement ☐ No ☐ I don't know

2. Is your organization unique in your community? (or at least not obviously duplicating the efforts of other agencies)?

   ☐ Yes ☐ Needs Improvement ☐ No ☐ I don't know

3. Is there a clear and critical need that can be explained in the appeal?

   ☐ Yes ☐ Needs Improvement ☐ No ☐ I don't know

4. Can you offer benefits to donors and/or show how their gift will make a difference?

   ☐ Yes ☐ Needs Improvement ☐ No ☐ I don't know

5. Do you have enough time and money to test your direct mail strategies thoroughly?

   ☐ Yes ☐ Needs Improvement ☐ No ☐ I don't know

6. Can you afford to lose your initial investment in direct mail?

   ☐ Yes ☐ Needs Improvement ☐ No ☐ I don't know

Is Your Organization Making Good Use of Direct Mail?

7. Do you keep your mailing lists up-to-date and clean?

   ☐ Yes ☐ Needs Improvement ☐ No ☐ I don't know

8. Do you trade mailing lists with other nonprofits?

   ☐ Yes ☐ Needs Improvement ☐ No ☐ I don't know

9. Do you know something about the people you are sending your solicitation letters to that leads you to believe they will be interested in your appeal?

   ☐ Yes ☐ Needs Improvement ☐ No ☐ I don't know

10. Do you test mailing lists, letters, and other components of your direct-mail packages before you invest in large mailings?

    ☐ Yes ☐ Needs Improvement ☐ No ☐ I don't know

11. Are your appeals carefully written and free of typos?

☐ Yes ☐ Needs Improvement ☐ No ☐ I don't know

12. Do your appeals specify the amount of the desired gift?

☐ Yes ☐ Needs Improvement ☐ No ☐ I don't know

13. Do they say what the gift will accomplish?

☐ Yes ☐ Needs Improvement ☐ No ☐ I don't know

14. Do you solicit regularly (at least twice each year)?

☐ Yes ☐ Needs Improvement ☐ No ☐ I don't know

15. Do you acknowledge gifts promptly?

☐ Yes ☐ Needs Improvement ☐ No ☐ I don't know

16. Do you have a mechanism for special treatment of "major donors"?

☐ Yes ☐ Needs Improvement ☐ No ☐ I don't know

17. Do you communicate with your donors/members regularly between solicitations?

☐ Yes ☐ Needs Improvement ☐ No ☐ I don't know

18. Are your cold-prospect mailings returning at least 1%?

☐ Yes ☐ Needs Improvement ☐ No ☐ I don't know

19. Do you get frequent complaints from solicitees?

☐ Yes ☐ Needs Improvement ☐ No ☐ I don't know

20. Do you analyze the results of each mailing to determine if it was cost-effective?

☐ Yes ☐ Needs Improvement ☐ No ☐ I don't know

This tool was used by:

_____

(Name/title)   (Date)

Fund development: Events

Discussion

Events can and should serve a dual function, raising money *and* promoting your organization. But even the ones that don't seem to cost anything are still expensive, requiring large investments of staff and volunteer time. These investments, and the concomitant risks of staff and volunteer burnout should be carefully considered when planning fundraising events.

1. Are your organization's events compatible with its mission? (Do they present the right image?)

   ☐ Yes ☐ Needs Improvement ☐ No ☐ I don't know

2. Are assignments for board, volunteers, and staff in line with their particular skills, abilities, and interests?

   ☐ Yes ☐ Needs Improvement ☐ No ☐ I don't know

3. Do you routinely explore sources of "in-kind" support (goods and services) in producing your events?

   ☐ Yes ☐ Needs Improvement ☐ No ☐ I don't know

4. Are the income objectives of events usually met?

   ☐ Yes ☐ Needs Improvement ☐ No ☐ I don't know

5. Other than money, are there measurable benefits to your organization from events?

   ☐ Yes ☐ Needs Improvement ☐ No ☐ I don't know

6. Do you usually get excited and look forward to your organization's events?

   ☐ Yes ☐ Needs Improvement ☐ No ☐ I don't know

7. Are you producing the right number of events each year?

   ☐ Yes ☐ Needs Improvement ☐ No ☐ I don't know

8. Is the amount of staff time invested in producing events for your organization commensurate with the economic and other returns?

   ☐ Yes ☐ Needs Improvement ☐ No ☐ I don't know

9. Do you usually feel satisfied afterwards?

   ☐ Yes ☐ Needs Improvement ☐ No ☐ I don't know

10. Are events evaluated soon afterward as an aid in planning the next?

    ☐ Yes ☐ Needs Improvement ☐ No ☐ I don't know

This tool was used by:

_____

(Name/title)   (Date)

Fund development: Special campaigns

INTRODUCTION

In many ways, capital and endowment campaigns draw on basic fundraising skills. Yet each requires some "special" skills and resources. More importantly, the added stress of a special campaign can be considerable. The following questions are aimed at helping you decide if your organization is ready to launch a special campaign with a reasonable likelihood of success.

This tool concludes with a brief series of questions on planned giving–a highly technical area of fund development. Planned giving programs, like direct-mail prospecting, are not for everyone. They require legal and financial planning expertise along with a high degree of sensitivity to donors and prospects. And the returns, although potentially great, are anything but quick.

All three of these special areas of fundraising should be undertaken cautiously and only after a thorough assessment of *your organization's strengths and proven capabilities.*

Note: Planning (or even contemplating) a capital or endowment campaign or planned giving program presents a good opportunity to inventory the skills, capabilities, and commitments of your board. It may also be a good time to recruit new members with special skills to help orchestrate the effort.

Capital and Endowment Campaigns: Discussion

Capital and endowment campaigns are extraordinary fundraising efforts, conducted on a limited timetable, geared toward raising funds for a specific purpose.

Generally, capital campaigns are undertaken to generate support for new buildings, renovation, and/or equipment purchases.

Endowment campaigns (sometimes undertaken along with a capital campaign) work to build a large fund of money that is kept intact. Endowments offer stability and, once built, are managed to maximize interest or dividend income. Although the endowment itself is restricted, the income it generates is available to the organization. Depending on the terms of the endowment, the income may be used for such purposes as program expenses, building maintenance, etc.

---

1. Is the image of your organization in the community strong? Does it inspire confidence?

   ☐ Yes ☐ Needs Improvement ☐ No ☐ I don't know

2. Does your agency have a solid long-range plan to guide its operations during the time of the special campaign?

   ☐ Yes ☐ Needs Improvement ☐ No ☐ I don't know

3. In your opinion, will the community and your constituencies easily see the need for your campaign?

   ☐ Yes ☐ Needs Improvement ☐ No ☐ I don't know

4. Is there general agreement on all levels of your organization about the need for and the appropriateness of the campaign at this time?

   ☐ Yes ☐ Needs Improvement ☐ No ☐ I don't know

5. Will your campaign have capable leadership both on the board and staff levels?

   ☐ Yes ☐ Needs Improvement ☐ No ☐ I don't know

6. Are you confident that your board chair and executive director can work together effectively as a team in connection with the campaign?

   ☐ Yes ☐ Needs Improvement ☐ No ☐ I don't know

7. Do you have a well-prepared team to carry out the various components of the campaign?

   ☐ Yes ☐ Needs Improvement ☐ No ☐ I don't know

8. As a whole, is your board prepared for its role in the special campaign? (Have the members made their own financial commitments? Do they possess the necessary skills and commitment to work on the campaign?)

   ☐ Yes ☐ Needs Improvement ☐ No ☐ I don't know

9. Does your board have the financial resources to play a leadership role in your capital or endowment campaign?

   ☐ Yes ☐ Needs Improvement ☐ No ☐ I don't know

10. Is your staff prepared for their role(s) in the special campaign?

    ☐ Yes ☐ Needs Improvement ☐ No ☐ I don't know

11. Do they understand the ultimate impact of the campaign on themselves?

    ☐ Yes ☐ Needs Improvement ☐ No ☐ I don't know

12. Is your existing donor base large enough to support your special campaign as well as your operations?

    ☐ Yes ☐ Needs Improvement ☐ No ☐ I don't know

13. Do you have reason to believe you can attract new donors to support your campaign?

    ☐ Yes ☐ Needs Improvement ☐ No ☐ I don't know

14. Do you have access to outside expertise if needed?

    ☐ Yes ☐ Needs Improvement ☐ No ☐ I don't know

15. Do you have sufficient resources to seed the campaign (e.g., pay for additional staff, consultants, printing, mailing, and other campaign costs)?

    ☐ Yes ☐ Needs Improvement ☐ No ☐ I don't know

16. Are your organization's operations (staffing, programs, board, and budget) stable enough to withstand the added strain of a special fundraising campaign?

    ☐ Yes ☐ Needs Improvement ☐ No ☐ I don't know

17. Do you have (or can you develop) the record keeping capabilities required for the successful administration of a capital or endowment campaign?

    ☐ Yes ☐ Needs Improvement ☐ No ☐ I don't know

18. Are you satisfied that the special campaign will be coordinated adequately with your organization's annual operating fund drive (i.e., that conflict and competition can be avoided)?

    ☐ Yes ☐ Needs Improvement ☐ No ☐ I don't know

19. Is your financial base strong enough (i.e., do you have sufficient cash reserves) to weather an initial negative impact on your operating fundraising because of your focus on the special campaign?

    ☐ Yes ☐ Needs Improvement ☐ No ☐ I don't know

20. Have you adequately considered the competition for contributions presented by other special campaigns in your area of service?

    ☐ Yes ☐ Needs Improvement ☐ No ☐ I don't know

21. Are you familiar with the experience of other organizations in your region and field of service regarding their capital or endowment campaign efforts?

    ☐ Yes ☐ Needs Improvement ☐ No ☐ I don't know

22. Do you feel you have enough information about the context for your campaign (e.g., the general state of the economy, the demographics of your region) so that you are confident about the community's ability to support your special campaign?

    ☐ Yes ☐ Needs Improvement ☐ No ☐ I don't know

23. Is there sufficient lead time to plan the campaign thoroughly?

    ☐ Yes ☐ Needs Improvement ☐ No ☐ I don't know

24. Are you planning specific gift opportunities that will offer major donors visibility and lasting acknowledgement?

    ☐ Yes ☐ Needs Improvement ☐ No ☐ I don't know

25. Are you confident that you will be able to attract one or more significant "kickoff" gifts in the earliest stages of your campaign?

    ☐ Yes ☐ Needs Improvement ☐ No ☐ I don't know

26. Does your campaign plan include appropriate acknowledgment to board, volunteers, and staff who work on the campaign?

    ☐ Yes ☐ Needs Improvement ☐ No ☐ I don't know

27. Based on your own past experience, do you have confidence in your ability to achieve the campaign goal?

    ☐ Yes ☐ Needs Improvement ☐ No ☐ I don't know

This tool was used by:

_____

(Name/title)   (Date)

Planned Giving: Discussion

Planned giving is an area of fund development that is getting more and more attention by a larger and larger number of nonprofits. The term is synonymous with "deferred gift" and simply means a gift planned for (or promised) now but delivered later. Later can mean at a specific date, or it can be upon the death of the donor. Cultivating these "promises" is sensitive business. It's also time-consuming, and the income realized by your organization may be decades away. Yet planned giving has captured the interest of many nonprofits. And the best gifts are ones where the donor and the organi.. both benefit. Embarking on a planned gifts progra. involves you in a complex maze of law, real estate, tax, and banking. It is rarely advisable to initiate a planned giving program without the help of experts in each of these areas.

Note: Experts say that the highest potential for planned gifts is from among an organization's existing donor base. Knowing those people well and assessing their ability to participate in your program is the first step.

---

1. Does your organization have a long and stable history of service?

   ☐ Yes ☐ Needs Improvement ☐ No ☐ I don't know

2. Are you convinced that the services your organization provides will continue to be needed long into the future?

   ☐ Yes ☐ Needs Improvement ☐ No ☐ I don't know

3. Is it clear to all who know of your organization that its effectiveness and longevity is not dependent on any single individual's leadership?

   ☐ Yes ☐ Needs Improvement ☐ No ☐ I don't know

4. Does your existing donor base have the potential to make planned gifts?

   ☐ Yes ☐ Needs Improvement ☐ No ☐ I don't know

5. Is your organization committed to the long-term potential benefits of planned giving (i.e., not in need of short-term success in this area)?

   ☐ Yes ☐ Needs Improvement ☐ No ☐ I don't know

6. Do you have (or are you willing to train) a competent planned giving officer on your staff?

   ☐ Yes ☐ Needs Improvement ☐ No ☐ I don't know

7. Do you have an attorney on staff or retainer to advise you about planned giving?

   ☐ Yes ☐ Needs Improvement ☐ No ☐ I don't know

8. Are you prepared to manage trust funds or property on behalf of your donors?

   ☐ Yes ☐ Needs Improvement ☐ No ☐ I don't know

9. Do you understand the pros and cons (for your organization as well as for your donors) of the charitable gift annuity?

   ☐ Yes ☐ Needs Improvement ☐ No ☐ I don't know

10. Have you investigated pooled income funds as a planned giving option for your donors?

    ☐ Yes ☐ Needs Improvement ☐ No ☐ I don't know

11. Do you know the difference between a charitable remainder unitrust and a charitable remainder annuity trust?

    ☐ Yes ☐ Needs Improvement ☐ No ☐ I don't know

12. Do you have established criteria for deciding which gifts to accept?

    ☐ Yes ☐ Needs Improvement ☐ No ☐ I don't know

This tool was used by:_____

(Name/title)   (Date)

FINANCIAL MANAGEMENT
Capabilities, systems, and reporting

INTRODUCTION

You might think that financial management is the same as bookkeeping. You might also think that (because numbers can simply be added up) assessing the strengths of your organization's financial management systems will be a snap. In some ways, this is true. Where money is concerned, the beginning of your analysis is quantifiable. But good financial management depends on communication as much as governance, fund development, or planning do.

Of course, you need a budget.

In fact, a budget is your organization's primary policy statement, reflecting your priorities in terms of the resources you allocate to them. But you won't be able to develop a useful, practical budget without a thorough understanding of programs and overall organizational goals.

Yet *budgeting* is just the beginning of financial management. Its complements are *record keeping, resource management, oversight,* and *reporting*.

Budgeting is a process of predicting the financial future of your organization, monitoring progress, and adjusting projections to reflect new information and revised assumptions on a periodic basis. Record keeping and oversight relate to handling cash transactions including documentation and approvals. Thorough documentation and control minimizes the cost of outside audits and the likelihood of undetected irregularities. Resource management, on the other hand, refers to the treasury function: how cash is invested and assets are managed. The reporting needs of your organization are of two kinds – internal and external. And reports support all of the other financial management functions.

Cash flow is a term we hear frequently. Nearly all nonprofits are concerned with it – and rightly so. Your organization will often receive grants on a reimbursement basis or be required to expend funds on a project well in advance of receiving fees for services.

An unrestricted cash reserve is the best solution to cash flow needs, but other means are often employed: A growing number of nonprofits have secured lines of credit or loans. These strategies can make a great deal of difference – offering your organization an opportunity to build its strength – as long as loans and lines of credit are not used as substitutes for income.

Finally, common sense enters into financial management. You can and should be able to understand budgets and financial statements. And record keeping should keep external reporting and development needs in mind in an effort to minimize the time needed to prepare special reports and budgets.

The following tool divides questions about financial management into three areas for assessment: Part I focuses on *capabilities*; Part II on *systems*, including record keeping, budgeting, oversight, and resource management; and Part III deals with *reporting*, both internal and external.

Note: People can be afraid of numbers. In your organization that may include your board chair or your executive director. Be sure people know how to use the budgets and statements prepared for them. A caution: Don't change your reporting format too often. When you do, you risk comparing apples with oranges and complicate long-term analyses and projections.

Financial management: Capabilities

Discussion

In this series of questions, we are concerned with the capabilities of the people within your organization regarding financial management. The term chief finan-cial officer (CFO) is used to refer to anyone who serves the function—even if he or she doesn't have that specific title. In fact, in most small to midsize nonprofits, the CFO function is filled by the executive director.

1. Is the person responsible for day-to-day financial management in your organization (the chief financial officer) prepared to fulfill the function competently?

   ☐ Yes ☐ Needs Improvement ☐ No ☐ I don't know

2. Is the CFO capable of explaining financial information and analyses to staff and board?

   ☐ Yes ☐ Needs Improvement ☐ No ☐ I don't know

3. Is your board treasurer capable and involved?

   ☐ Yes ☐ Needs Improvement ☐ No ☐ I don't know

4. If your organization has a finance committee, is it effective?

   ☐ Yes ☐ Needs Improvement ☐ No ☐ I don't know

5. In general, do board and staff members understand budgets and financial statements?

   ☐ Yes ☐ Needs Improvement ☐ No ☐ I don't know

This tool was used by:

_____

(Name/title)   (date)

Financial management: Systems

Discussion

The following questions about your organization's financial systems are divided into four subgroups: record keeping, budgeting, oversight, and resource management.

Note: These questions are a good beginning for you in assessing basic financial management systems. Whether your books are kept manually or on computer, the complexity of the record keeping and reporting will vary, depending on the size and complexity of your organization.

Record keeping

1. Is your organization's chart of accounts detailed enough?

   ☐ Yes ☐ Needs Improvement ☐ No ☐ I don't know

2. Do you have an adequate system for recording non-cash or in-kind contributions?

   ☐ Yes ☐ Needs Improvement ☐ No ☐ I don't know

3. Do you have an adequate system for matching restricted gifts or grants to related program expenses?

   ☐ Yes ☐ Needs Improvement ☐ No ☐ I don't know

4. Do you have an up-to-date inventory of fixed assets (e.g., buildings and equipment)?

   ☐ Yes ☐ Needs Improvement ☐ No ☐ I don't know

5. Are expense requests documented (e.g., accompanied by receipts or invoices)?

   ☐ Yes ☐ Needs Improvement ☐ No ☐ I don't know

Budgeting

6. Do budget categories mirror your organization's chart of accounts?

   ☐ Yes ☐ Needs Improvement ☐ No ☐ I don't know

7. In general, do you feel that revenue projections made for your organization are realistic? (Are increases in budgeted income supported by detailed strategies for achieving those income goals?)

   ☐ Yes ☐ Needs Improvement ☐ No ☐ I don't know

8. Are expense projections made so as to contain costs as much as possible?

   ☐ Yes ☐ Needs Improvement ☐ No ☐ I don't know

9. Are financial goals developed with input from your fundraising staff as well as program personnel and board?

   ☐ Yes ☐ Needs Improvement ☐ No ☐ I don't know

10. Are draft budgets prepared and circulated well enough in advance of the new fiscal year to enable full discussion and analysis before the budget is adopted?

    ☐ Yes ☐ Needs Improvement ☐ No ☐ I don't know

11. Are budgets ready in a timely manner to support development efforts?

    ☐ Yes ☐ Needs Improvement ☐ No ☐ I don't know

12. Do you refer to actual income and expenses of prior years in preparing budget projections?

    ☐ Yes ☐ Needs Improvement ☐ No ☐ I don't know

13. Does your budget break out program related costs from administration/overhead?

    ☐ Yes ☐ Needs Improvement ☐ No ☐ I don't know

14. Is cash flow projected regularly enough?

    ☐ Yes ☐ Needs Improvement ☐ No ☐ I don't know

Oversight

15. Is there good communication about financial matters between staff and board?

    ☐ Yes ☐ Needs Improvement ☐ No ☐ I don't know

16. Is enough time spent at board and committee meetings reviewing and analyzing budgets and financial statements?

    ☐ Yes ☐ Needs Improvement ☐ No ☐ I don't know

17. Are budget projections and actual income and expenses compared periodically to aid in making adjustments?

    ☐ Yes ☐ Needs Improvement ☐ No ☐ I don't know

18. Are internal controls sufficient to ensure that the budgeted costs are not exceeded without careful analysis and approval?

    ☐ Yes ☐ Needs Improvement ☐ No ☐ I don't know

19. Are payroll taxes withheld and paid to the IRS regularly and promptly according to law?

    ☐ Yes ☐ Needs Improvement ☐ No ☐ I don't know

20. Are expenditure approvals subject to an independent review to ensure appropriateness (e.g., counter-signatures, authorizations)?

    ☐ Yes ☐ Needs Improvement ☐ No ☐ I don't know

21. Are the financial controls in your organization adequate to minimize the likelihood of misappropriation of funds?

    ☐ Yes ☐ Needs Improvement ☐ No ☐ I don't know

22. If your organization has a deficit, is there an adequate plan in place to retire it?

    ☐ Yes ☐ Needs Improvement ☐ No ☐ I don't know

Resource Management

23. Is surplus cash invested appropriately (conservatively, in line with fiduciary responsibilities and effectively, to maximize return)?

    ☐ Yes ☐ Needs Improvement ☐ No ☐ I don't know

24. Do you have adequate means/resources for managing cash flow (e.g., cash reserve, line of credit)?

    ☐ Yes ☐ Needs Improvement ☐ No ☐ I don't know

25. Do you have adequate insurance coverage and maintenance provisions for your building and equipment?

    ☐ Yes ☐ Needs Improvement ☐ No ☐ I don't know

This tool was used by:

_____

(Name/title)   (date)

Financial management: Reporting

1. Are reports clear and easy to read?

   ☐ Yes   ☐ Needs Improvement   ☐ No   ☐ I don't know

2. Are reports comparative (i.e., budget versus actual; current versus prior accounting period)?

   ☐ Yes   ☐ Needs Improvement   ☐ No   ☐ I don't know

3. Are financial reports thorough without being overly detailed?

   ☐ Yes   ☐ Needs Improvement   ☐ No   ☐ I don't know

4. Is financial information summarized and presented for the board and executive management clearly and in a timely manner?

   ☐ Yes   ☐ Needs Improvement   ☐ No   ☐ I don't know

5. Are complete reports to funders, the IRS, state tax authorities, and regulatory agencies prepared on time?

   ☐ Yes   ☐ Needs Improvement   ☐ No   ☐ I don't know

6. Do you make use of fund accounting principles where appropriate?

   ☐ Yes   ☐ Needs Improvement   ☐ No   ☐ I don't know

This tool was used by:

_____

(Name/title)   (date)

PUBLIC RELATIONS AND MARKETING

INTRODUCTION

Usually when we say all in one breath, "public-relations-and-marketing," we link two very different and highly technical aspects of the work of a nonprofit. When managers are asked about either or both, they generally mumble things like, "linking," "image building," "developing support," "newspaper coverage," "selling the organization," "advertising," and – paradoxically – "everything but advertising."

It's possible they are all talking about basically the same kinds of activities and benefits. But it's also possible they aren't. So, we'll introduce each part of this tool with a little excursion into semantic clarification.

Note: There is tremendous overlap in the implementation of public relations and marketing campaigns. Be aware that many marketing efforts build public awareness and many public relations activities will support and bolster marketing efforts.

Public relations and marketing: Public relations

Discussion

Public relations is time consuming and rarely has a direct financial reward. But good relations with your publics are essential. Without public awareness of your organization and sympathy for its cause, fundraising, membership, and even board development efforts will fall flat.

Professionals in the PR business separate it into media relations and other public relations. *Media rela-*

tions describes itself pretty well. It involves communicating and developing relationships with professionals in the media (from newspaper and magazines to radio and television). Nonprofits get a great deal of attention from the media without paying for it through news coverage and public services announcements, if they pursue it.

The rest of public relations includes anything and everything undertaken to develop awareness of and sympathy for an organization and its cause.

---

1. Do you believe your organization projects a consistent public image?

   ☐ Yes ☐ Needs Improvement ☐ No ☐ I don't know

2. Does your name and logo appropriately identify your organization and its purpose?

   ☐ Yes ☐ Needs Improvement ☐ No ☐ I don't know

3. Do you have good working relationships with representatives of the major periodicals published in your region?

   ☐ Yes ☐ Needs Improvement ☐ No ☐ I don't know

4. Is your organization mentioned frequently enough in the media?

   ☐ Yes ☐ Needs Improvement ☐ No ☐ I don't know

5. Is your executive director a good spokesperson for your organization?

   ☐ Yes ☐ Needs Improvement ☐ No ☐ I don't know

6. Does he or she spend the right amount of time out of the office at public meetings, conferences, and the like?

   ☐ Yes ☐ Needs Improvement ☐ No ☐ I don't know

7. Does your board of directors include well-respected members of the community who speak readily and positively about your organization and its programs?

   ☐ Yes ☐ Needs Improvement ☐ No ☐ I don't know

8. Do you communicate with your supporters regularly enough?

   ☐ Yes ☐ Needs Improvement ☐ No ☐ I don't know

9. Do your special events or fundraising benefits enhance your organization's image in the community?

   ☐ Yes ☐ Needs Improvement ☐ No ☐ I don't know

This tool was used by:

_____

(Name/title)   (date)

Public relations and marketing: Marketing

Discussion

Whether you're cultivating donors, looking for members, or selling theater tickets, you need to know the basic principles of marketing. To begin with, marketing is not selling. In fact, the two terms stand in diametric opposition: *selling* focuses on the needs of the organization — "Subscribe to *our* theater," "Contribute to *our* cause." *Marketing*, on the other hand, focuses on the consumer/ prospect's needs. "*Your*" values are of primary importance to our organization; join others like yourself..."

So if you decide to *market* your organization, you need to know your current and prospective supporters.

The following series of questions will help you assess your familiarity with your constituents and also with basic marketing concepts.

---

1. Is your visual image consistent? (Is it easy to identify your organization with all your publications and printed materials?)

   ☐ Yes ☐ Needs Improvement ☐ No ☐ I don't know

2. Are your reasonably sure you know *why* people volunteer time or donate money to your organization?

   ☐ Yes ☐ Needs Improvement ☐ No ☐ I don't know

3. Do your supporters and constituents rate your organization's programs and services highly?

   ☐ Yes ☐ Needs Improvement ☐ No ☐ I don't know

4. If you have a membership, do you know its demographics?

   ☐ Yes ☐ Needs Improvement ☐ No ☐ I don't know

5. If you have a membership, have you surveyed it recently enough?

   ☐ Yes ☐ Needs Improvement ☐ No ☐ I don't know

6. Before conducting a survey, do you get agreement about why you are conducting it and what problems it is intended to address?

   ☐ Yes ☐ Needs Improvement ☐ No ☐ I don't know

7. Do you think your members, constituent groups, and the general public have the same view of your organization's strengths?

   ☐ Yes ☐ Needs Improvement ☐ No ☐ I don't know

8. Do you know your competition well (e.g., other organizations that provide similar services in region?)

   ☐ Yes ☐ Needs Improvement ☐ No ☐ I don't know

9. Can you distinguish your organization's attributes from those of competing organizations?

   ☐ Yes ☐ Needs Improvement ☐ No ☐ I don't know

10. Are those distinctions easily communicated to your members, constituents, and potential supporters?

    ☐ Yes ☐ Needs Improvement ☐ No ☐ I don't know

11. If there are several organizations in your region providing similar services, are you sure your programs and services are competitive (e.g., high quality, cost-effective, well respected)?

    ☐ Yes ☐ Needs Improvement ☐ No ☐ I don't know

12. Do you devote adequate resources to market research and marketing?

    ☐ Yes ☐ Needs Improvement ☐ No ☐ I don't know

13. Are you aware of social and political trends in your region and nationally that may affect the success of your marketing efforts?

    ☐ Yes ☐ Needs Improvement ☐ No ☐ I don't know

This tool was used by:

_____

(Name/title)   (date)

QUALITY ASSURANCE

INTRODUCTION

If you are reading this volume from front to back, you're arriving at the beginning just as you thought you were coming to the end.

Quality in programs and services is the *result* of a well-run and -managed organization with strong purpose, leadership, skill, and commitment. It is also the *reason* for your agency's very existence—your most important organizational goal. In fact, if we cannot document that we are doing a job well, we risk losing financial and political support. And none of us has any business using resources unless we're reasonably sure we're doing some good. Being "reasonably sure" is what quality assurance is all about.

> A comprehensive—and sensible—approach to quality assurance can improve policymaking, planning, program development, service delivery, and accountability for your agency.

At its most effective, quality assurance will involve many people throughout your organization who will develop the standards to evaluate your programs. Your challenge is to make certain that these standards demand excellence, rather than a minimum acceptable level of performance.

Step one in creating a comprehensive quality assurance system for your agency is setting standards that will make it possible for you to measure (and improve) your performance. Standards can be set to help measure *capability; good practice; what you produce* with your resources; and, finally, the *effect* of your services.

For example, your capability can be measured by the qualifications of your program staff as well as the physical resources you are able to allocate to your programs. Setting standards for good practice is a way of talking about your agency's process and procedures for delivering service. This is less quantifiable than counting the number of people served, but we all know that quality and quantity are not the same thing when dealing with human needs and human services. Finally, standards which help in measuring the outcome of your services will involve tracking, follow-up, and perhaps also the client's own evaluation of how you helped them.

Quality assurance systems can be built on national or state standards, applying to whole systems of agencies, or they can be unique and personal to a single organization, intended to enhance the implementation of a single individual's vision. In the case of a statewide system of human service agencies, quality assurance may be linked by the state regulatory or funding agency. Or, in the case of a regional theater, quality may be measured against a standard of critical acclaim or peer review.

The following series of questions offers you a place to begin in considering the assurance of quality as an integral part of your organization's capabilities, practice, and impact. We would also recommend that you peruse (or revisit) the tool on planning. Be alert to quality as part and parcel of a healthy successful nonprofit. Because a system of quality assurance relates to almost every area of agency operations, quality assurance can be seen as threatening—another area where fear of change must be acknowledged and dealt with constructively in your agency.

QUESTIONS

1. Are the problems you are addressing the same ones as those that instigated the founding of your organization?

   ☐ Yes ☐ Needs Improvement ☐ No ☐ I don't know

2. Are the services your agency provides consistent with demonstrable needs?

   ☐ Yes ☐ Needs Improvement ☐ No ☐ I don't know

3. Do you have a thorough understanding of the program delivery systems in your agency?

   ☐ Yes ☐ Needs Improvement ☐ No ☐ I don't know

4. Do the committees to programs actually produce an acceptable level and quality of service?

   ☐ Yes ☐ Needs Improvement ☐ No ☐ I don't know

5. Does your organization share a common vision of quality?

   ☐ Yes ☐ Needs Improvement ☐ No ☐ I don't know

6. Is there a commitment to quality throughout your agency?

   ☐ Yes ☐ Needs Improvement ☐ No ☐ I don't know

7. Do you develop standards for assuring quality collaboratively, involving representatives from all levels of your organization (from client to board members)?

   ☐ Yes ☐ Needs Improvement ☐ No ☐ I don't know

8. Does your agency have agreed-upon standards regarding the quality as well as the quantity of service you wish to provide?

   ☐ Yes ☐ Needs Improvement ☐ No ☐ I don't know

9. In setting standards for quality in performance, does your agency look at internal goals as well as objective standards set by regulatory agencies?

   ☐ Yes ☐ Needs Improvement ☐ No ☐ I don't know

10. Do your standards describe quality without setting unrealistic goals or creating unrealistic expectations?

    ☐ Yes ☐ Needs Improvement ☐ No ☐ I don't know

11. Is your actual performance reviewed against these standards?

    ☐ Yes ☐ Needs Improvement ☐ No ☐ I don't know

12. Does your system of assuring quality build on practices already in place?

    ☐ Yes ☐ Needs Improvement ☐ No ☐ I don't know

13. Are your mechanisms for monitoring performance thorough without being burdensome?

    ☐ Yes ☐ Needs Improvement ☐ No ☐ I don't know

14. Are you taking steps to avoid unnecessary duplication and overlap in measuring performance?

    ☐ Yes ☐ Needs Improvement ☐ No ☐ I don't know

15. Do you review your standards and measurement mechanisms frequently enough to ensure continued relevance?

    ☐ Yes ☐ Needs Improvement ☐ No ☐ I don't know

16. Are your program staff adequately prepared to provide services according to your standards for quality?

    ☐ Yes ☐ Needs Improvement ☐ No ☐ I don't know

17. Is there clear communication about what is expected in terms of job performance?

    ☐ Yes ☐ Needs Improvement ☐ No ☐ I don't know

18. Are there mechanisms in your agency that support quality (e.g., reinforcement, encouragement, incentives)?

    ☐ Yes ☐ Needs Improvement ☐ No ☐ I don't know

19. Do you follow through on program enhancements?

    ☐ Yes ☐ Needs Improvement ☐ No ☐ I don't know

20. Do the services your agency provides produce the intended effects?

    ☐ Yes ☐ Needs Improvement ☐ No ☐ I don't know

21. Is evaluation of the quality of your program delivery tied appropriately to your agency's planning process?

    ☐ Yes ☐ Needs Improvement ☐ No ☐ I don't know

This tool was used by:

_____

(Name/title)   (date)

ABOUT THE AUTHORS

Barbara Kibbe is a management consultant who works exclusively with nonprofit organizations, offering them a range of services from organizational assessment and strategic planning to mediation and program evaluation. She is a principal in Harder & Kibbe Research and Consulting in San Francisco. Their clients include health, human service, educational, and cultural organizations ranging from small and emerging groups to institutions with annual budgets in excess of $20 million. Barbara's background includes a law degree and training in fundraising, personnel management, painting, and carpentry.

Fred Setterberg's work has appeared in a wide variety of publications, including *The Nation, Mother Jones, Reader's Digest, The Utne Reader, Psychology Today,* and others. He is the coauthor, with Kary Schulman, of *Beyond Profit: The Complete Guide to Managing the Nonprofit Organization* (Harper & Row, 1985). A book of his essays on American writers and landscapes will be published next year by John Daniel and Company. He is currently working with Lonny Shavelson on a book about the chemical contamination of American towns to be published by John Wiley and Sons. Fred is a contributing editor with Pacific News Service in San Francisco.

ABOUT THE PACKARD FOUNDATION'S
MANAGEMENT ASSISTANCE PROGRAM

The David and Lucile Packard Foundation's Management Assistance Program was established in 1984 to enable nonprofit organizations to improve and strengthen their management capabilities. This program is conducted with the belief that, in most cases, improved management contributes to increased effectiveness in the accomplishment of an organization's own purpose and goals, and thus strengthens the organization's ability to make a positive contribution to its community.

There are a variety of different forms which could be designated as management assistance, including outside consulting services, trainings and workshops, classes, and clinics that wed theory and practice. It is our belief that when carefully selected and judiciously used, management assistance can enable an organization to address its needs, transform problems into opportunities, and help an organization's leaders more effectively manage the ongoing process of change.

For the most part, the foundation's grantmaking in this program area has been divided into support of individual grantee organizations and support of those entities delivering services or producing products intended to improve management effectiveness within the nonprofit sector. With respect to funding of individual organizations, the foundation supports the consulting fees and expenses relating to the management intervention of grantees when the project is directed to long-term growth. Grants are made to help pay for consultation and training in such areas as strategic planning, evaluation and monitoring, board development, fundraising, marketing, organizational development, and other management areas leading to increased effectiveness.

The second component of this program relates to helping to improve or build capacity within the nonprofit sector. The foundation invests in management support organizations (generally local) that provide low-cost training and consulting assistance. Grants have also been made to develop and implement projects leading to management improvement for the purpose of creating new and useful materials or programs.